Machiavelli

For over four hundred years, *The Prince* has been the basic handbook of politics, statesmanship, and power. Written by a Florentine nobleman whose name has become a synonym for crafty plotting, it is a fascinating political and social document, as pertinent today as when it first appeared. Machiavelli wanted to set down for all time the rules and moves in the ageless game of politics, and, as the most successful statesman of his day, he devised this highly readable formula for the man who seeks power. There was little modern democracy in sixteenth century Italy, and as a result, Machiavelli's work became thought of as a blueprint for dictators—instead of a guide for efficient democratic government.

Witty, informative and devilishly shrewd, Machiavelli has long been required reading for everyone interested in politics and power. *The Prince* is one of the significant books of all time.

CHRISTIAN GAUSS, the late Dean Emeritus of Princeton University, has written a new and penetrating introduction to this MENTOR edition, explaining the times in which Machiavelli lived and the meaning of the book to today's reader. Dean Gauss, who died shortly after completing this analysis, was a noted American liberal educator and scholar.

THIS BOOK IS A REPRINT OF THE ORIGINAL HARD-COVER EDITION PUBLISHED BY THE OXFORD UNIVERSITY PRESS

Niccolò Machiavelli

The PRINCE

Introduction by Christian Gauss

The Oxford University Press "World's Classics" translation by Luigi Ricci, revised by E. R. P. Vincent.

A MENTOR BOOK

NEW AMERICAN LIBRARY

NEW YORK AND SCARBOROUGH, ONTARIO

MENTOR TRADEMARK REG. U.S. PAT. OFF. AND FOREIGN COUNTRIES
REGISTERED TRADEMARK—MARCA REGISTRADA
HECHO EN CHICAGO, U.S.A.

SIGNET, SIGNET CLASSIC, MENTOR, ONYX, PLUME, MERIDIAN AND
NAL BOOKS are published *in the United States* by
NAL PENGUIN INC.,
1633 Broadway, New York, New York 10019,
in Canada by The New American Library of Canada Limited,
81 Mack Avenue, Scarborough, Ontario M1L 1M8

35 36 37 38 39 40 41 42 43

PRINTED IN THE UNITED STATES OF AMERICA

CONTENTS

Introduction to the MENTOR Edition
by Christian Gauss   7

1. THE VARIOUS KINDS OF GOVERNMENT AND THE WAYS BY WHICH THEY ARE ESTABLISHED   33

2. OF HEREDITARY MONARCHIES   34

3. OF MIXED MONARCHIES   35

4. WHY THE KINGDOM OF DARIUS, OCCUPIED BY ALEXANDER, DID NOT REBEL AGAINST THE SUCCESSORS OF THE LATTER AFTER HIS DEATH   43

5. THE WAY TO GOVERN CITIES OR DOMINIONS THAT, PREVIOUS TO BEING OCCUPIED, LIVED UNDER THEIR OWN LAWS   46

6. OF NEW DOMINIONS WHICH HAVE BEEN ACQUIRED BY ONE'S OWN ARMS AND ABILITY   48

7. OF NEW DOMINIONS ACQUIRED BY THE POWER OF OTHERS OR BY FORTUNE   52

8. OF THOSE WHO HAVE ATTAINED THE POSITION OF PRINCE BY VILLAINY   59

9. OF THE CIVIC PRINCIPALITY   63

10. HOW THE STRENGTH OF ALL STATES SHOULD BE MEASURED   67

11. OF ECCLESIASTICAL PRINCIPALITIES   69

12. THE DIFFERENT KINDS OF MILITIA AND MERCENARY SOLDIERS 72

13. OF AUXILIARY, MIXED, AND NATIVE TROOPS 77

14. THE DUTIES OF A PRINCE WITH REGARD TO THE MILITIA 81

15. OF THE THINGS FOR WHICH MEN, AND ESPECIALLY PRINCES, ARE PRAISED OR BLAMED 84

16. OF LIBERALITY AND NIGGARDLINESS 86

17. OF CRUELTY AND CLEMENCY, AND WHETHER IT IS BETTER TO BE LOVED OR FEARED 89

18. IN WHAT WAY PRINCES MUST KEEP FAITH 92

19. THAT WE MUST AVOID BEING DESPISED AND HATED 95

20. WHETHER FORTRESSES AND OTHER THINGS WHICH PRINCES OFTEN CONTRIVE ARE USEFUL OR INJURIOUS 105

21. HOW A PRINCE MUST ACT IN ORDER TO GAIN REPUTATION 110

22. OF THE SECRETARIES OF PRINCES 114

23. HOW FLATTERERS MUST BE SHUNNED 116

24. WHY THE PRINCES OF ITALY HAVE LOST THEIR STATES 118

25. HOW MUCH FORTUNE CAN DO IN HUMAN AFFAIRS AND HOW IT MAY BE OPPOSED 120

26. EXHORTATION TO LIBERATE ITALY FROM THE BARBARIANS 124

Introduction to the Mentor Edition

by CHRISTIAN GAUSS

I

FIFTY YEARS AGO, if the average American reader or the student in the American college picked up Machiavelli's *Prince* at all, he did so out of sheer curiosity. For him it was an outmoded book. The very title was against it. The age of kings and princes was passing. He knew that the treatise had been written in the period which the most widely read of the English historians of the Renaissance, J. A. Symonds, called *The Age of the Despots*, and Machiavelli himself, in quite general acceptation, bore so unsavory a reputation that the word "Machiavellian" had become imbedded in our language as synonymous with Mephistophelian. On the strength of a famous essay of Macaulay's, the notion had become fairly widespread that the devil himself had become familiarly known as the Old Nick only because Niccolò had been Machiavelli's first name.

Why, in many quarters, the reputation of Machiavelli and his *Prince* went into eclipse must be explained later. But it is safe to say that in America, as elsewhere, no book has undergone so favorable a reversal of fortune. Newer interpretations of history, the emergence in the twentieth century of new types of states and the clashes between them may help to explain why *The Prince* has again become required reading for us all. Probably no single brief book, certainly no other book of that time, will put the twentieth-century reader so immediately in touch with some of the central problems of our day. These central problems have to do with what is, or what should be, the relation of the citizen to the state, and what is, or what should be, the relation of the states to each other, and what are the sources of, and the limits, if any, to the power of the state. In addition to its brevity, there are stylistic qualities in *The Prince* which make it easy if not delightful reading. Unlike that later diplomat, Talleyrand, Machiavelli never uses words to conceal his thought. His meaning is never ambiguous. His conclusions may occasionally be unwelcome but they are always as downright as a box on the ear, and it is safe to predict that for the modern reader he will set some of the problems of citizenship, statecraft and political power into new and sharper focus.

We shall also see later that Machiavelli too could have said that it was "a condition and not a theory" which confronted him. His book, therefore, is not an abstract treatise; it is a concise manual, a handbook for those who would acquire or increase their political power. As such it has a history of study and use by a long line of kings and ministers as diverse in aims and character as Richelieu, Christina of Sweden, Frederick of Prussia, Bismarck and Clemenceau. In these cases they all possessed recognized credentials to power. In the twentieth century this circle has been widely extended by those in revolt against the older forms of the state. In his student days Mussolini selected it as the subject of a thesis for his doctorate. It was Hitler's bedside reading, and we need not be taken aback when in his excellent introduction to *The Prince* and *The Discourses* Max Lerner tells us that Lenin and Stalin as well have gone to school to Machiavelli.

It is of course true that a good book, like a sound scientific discovery, may be put to humanly undesirable uses without vitiating its central truth. Even if dispassionate investigation should disclose that holders of political power in democracies like our own in this period of instability are more frequently using methods once condemned as "Machiavellian," it would prove little. We are here concerned primarily with one of the major tensions in our culture. No one in our time can fail to note the rise to power of new political leaders like Lenin and Stalin, Mussolini and Hitler, who at times openly proclaim and at others do not conceal that they believe salvation can only come through the greatly increased power of the national state. On the other hand, no one can fail to note in many quarters an earnest effort to create what Wendell Willkie called *One World*. The United Nations is a more determined attempt to create a "super-state" which to succeed must have at least some power in the interest of peace and human welfare. This is still a major tension of our time. In the last fifty years Machiavelli has repeatedly been hailed as the founder of modern political science. Historians as distinguished as Ranke and Meinecke in Germany, and Lord Acton in England, find in Machiavelli one of the founders of modern historical analysis. A reconsideration of Machiavelli and the steadily increasing favor with which *The Prince* is being regarded may therefore throw some light on the origin if not the solution of our major political problems.

II

MACHIAVELLI'S OWN WORK is all the more deeply rooted in his own time since he was not in the first instance a writer or theorist but an active participant in the troubled and unstable political life of his native Florence.

He was born there in 1469, the descendant of an old Tuscan family. An earlier member of the family had actively opposed the rise of the Medici bankers to power and had died in prison for his pains. The Medici had established a relatively mild despotism which, while allowing older republican forms to persist, retained for themselves the substance of power. None of the Machiavellis favored the Medici. Niccolò's father was a lawyer, and both father and son regarded themselves as republicans. We know little about the details of his education but it is plain that it was that of the humanist of his time, that he found his ideals in Rome and read the works of the Greeks in Latin translations.

Machiavelli grew up under the rule of that member of the Medici dynasty to whom the Florentines have

given the title Lorenzo the Magnificent, and the Age of
Lorenzo has often been described as the Augustan Age of
the Italian Renaissance. Lorenzo himself was a distinguished humanist and poet and generous patron of ar-
tists and scholars. He has been credited with maintaining
a sort of balance of power between the five major Italian
units of power—the Kingdom of Naples, Rome and the
papal state, Venice, Florence and Milan. But it should be
remembered that during the period of his rule (1469-
1492) his brother was assassinated and he himself
wounded in the conspiracy of a rival faction, and that
these five units were themselves unstable. They were
engaged in continual struggles with lesser cities, as Florence was with Pisa, which often resulted in open warfare.
The balance of power was, therefore, so shifting and
precarious that a shrewd observer like Machiavelli could
have had no illusions about his city's having found a
solution to its political problems. Lorenzo died in
1492. His successor Piero was exiled two years later when
a new peril, the French army under Charles VIII, appeared in Florence. The Dominican monk Savonarola,
after he had reformed the republic and almost succeeded
in establishing a theocracy, was executed and burned in
1498. Some months later Machiavelli was elected Secre-
tary to the Second Chancery of the Republic of Florence,
which had charge of foreign and military affairs. He was
influential in shaping policy and there could be no
higher tribute to his political competence than the fact
that he was sent on twenty-four missions, including four
to the King of France, several to Rome and one to the
Emperor Maximilian. After thirteen years of service, another turn of the political kaleidoscope brought the
French army back to Florence. The Florentines, in panic,
recalled the Medici, and Machiavelli in his turn was
exiled.

Machiavelli had been an able, conscientious public
servant of the republic. The conditions of his exile condemned him for a time to live on a small property which
he owned in the country and forbade him to set foot in

Florence. He has himself described this reversal of fortune in a letter to his friend Vettori:

> *I am living in the country since my disgrace. I get up*
> *at dawn and go to the little wood where I see what*
> *work has been done* (by the woodcutters). *After gos-*
> siping with them he withdrew to a hill to read Dante
> or Petrarch, Tibullus or Ovid. Then after his frugal
> midday meal he went to the inn to talk with the miller,
> the landlord, the butcher and a couple of bricklayers
> and spent the afternoon *with these boors playing cards*
> *or dice; we quarrel over farthings. When evening comes*
> *I return to the house and go into my study. Before I*
> *enter I take off my rough mud-stained country dress.*
> *I put on my royal and curial robes and thus fittingly*
> *attired I enter into the assembly of men of old times.*
> *Welcomed by them I feed upon that food which is my*
> *true nourishment, and which has made me what I am.*
> *I dare to talk with them, and ask them the reason for*
> *their actions. Of their kindness they answer me. I no*
> *longer fear poverty or death. . . . From these notes I*
> *have composed a little work,* The Prince.

It was his intention to dedicate it to one of the Medici in the hope that they might invite him back to public service. He did write a letter of dedication to the new Lorenzo but it remains doubtful whether it was ever presented to him before his death in 1519. It is certain that *The Prince* was circulated in manuscript and plagiarized, but it was not published until five years after Machiavelli's death in 1532.

In his later years, thanks to friends and organizations in Florence, he was sent on minor missions, and thanks to the influence of Cardinal di Medici (later Pope Clement VII) he was commissioned to write *The History of Florence* with a small annual salary.

By this time new factors had further complicated the problems of Italy and added to her dissensions and to Machiavelli's unhappiness. Luther started the Reformation, and the rivalry of the new German emperor Charles

V and Francis I of France for dominion in Italy resulted
in the Sack of Rome and another expulsion of the Medici
in 1527.

III

The Prince does not give us the whole of Machiavelli's
political thinking. It treated the most acute problem of
Italy, its inferiority in political organization and military strength to nearby states like Spain and France and
was addressed to princes like the Medici, to whom it
was dedicated. The fact that he took no steps to pub-
lish it in his lifetime, even after it was plagiarized, supports this view. It need not astonish us to recall that
it became a handbook for aspirants to political power,
and that when in the twentieth century nation states
themselves ran into a period of instability it should again
have been studied both by idealists and by political ad-
venturers. For Machiavelli's reputation it is unfortunate
that it so rapidly overshadowed all his work and became
the one book upon which his reputation rests.

Within twenty years of its publication, it had passed
through twenty-five editions. If there is any one hero of
The Prince, it is Cesare Borgia, whose achievements received such admiring commendations in Chapter 7. This
is because, to Machiavelli, as later to Garibaldi, the ex-
istence of an ecclesiastical state in central Italy would
always remain a barrier to her political unification. With
tacit consent, and at times active assistance, from his
father the Pope, Alexander VI, Cesare was making this
area a strong political domain of his own and would, so
Machiavelli believed, with a little better fortune, have
created a center around which the new Italy might co-
alesce. After the Medici provided cardinals and popes to
the Church, Machiavelli hoped that this same process of
creating a central Italian state might be resumed with
greater success by the coordination of Medici power in
Florence and in Rome.

From the standpoint of his later reputation, time was
to prove that Machiavelli had made one of his gravest
errors in the choice of his hero. Cesare had committed

crimes on his way to power, and it might be added that he had committed other crimes quite incidentally as well. But it is also true on the testimony of other contemporary historians in his domains, and it is worth remembering, that he had appointed as director of public works an engineer of no mean ability, Leonardo da Vinci. There was another reason why Cesare's prowess appealed to Machiavelli. It will be recalled that during his public service Machiavelli was concerned with military affairs also. Here he early became convinced that the employment of mercenaries by Florence and Italian cities generally would never provide an adequate and reliable military force. Cesare, with the improvement of the lot of the people in his Romagna, had raised and trained his own native levies, a plan which Machiavelli himself had followed. Even so, the text itself of the famous Chapter 7 indicates that Machiavelli was conscious that he was inviting disapproval in making Cesare his hero. That, I believe, is the reason why he felt called upon to repeat: "Reviewing thus all the actions of the Duke (Cesare Borgia), I find nothing to blame, on the contrary I feel bound, as I have done, to hold him up as an example to be imitated by all who by fortune and with the arms of others have risen to power."

But the moral climate of Europe and of Italy was to change rapidly, and within fifty years the son of a Pope, particularly this son of a Borgia Pope, would no longer be acceptable as a model for the savior of Italy. There were other objections also, particularly the glorification of the qualities of the lion and the fox, of force and fraud.

It was for this reason that the immediate effects of Machiavelli's *Prince* on Italian politics were almost nil. Rome, though it alleged other reasons, placed it on the Index of Prohibited Books in 1559. The Inquisition decreed the utter destruction of all Machiavelli's works, and this was confirmed by the Council of Trent. In 1576 a French Huguenot wrote a violent refutation of *The Prince* which was widely circulated and translated into English.

For English readers the rapidity with which Machia-

velli's reputation spread is indicated by the frequency
with which his name appears as a byword in the work
of the Elizabethan dramatists. It is true that the Machiavelli who speaks the prologue in Marlowe's *Jew of
Malta* is a travesty. An able American scholar, Hardin
Craig, proved, however, that the older assumption that
all these dramatists could have had no first-hand ac-
quaintance with Machiavelli is no longer tenable. Beside
a Latin and three French published translations it is
now plain that English translations as well circulated in
manuscript. When in *The Merry Wives of Windsor*
Shakespeare has one of his characters ask: "Am I subtle?
Am I a Machiavel?" it is plain that he intended no com-
pliment. The general tenor of all these references can
be summed up in one from Marston's *Pygmalion:* "A
damned Machiavellian holds candle to the devil for
a while."

This should be sufficient to indicate that in England
as well as in France and Spain and Italy, within sev-
enty-five years of the publication of *The Prince,* Machiavelli's name had already been taken over into ordinary speech with those connotations which we have
already mentioned. Machiavelli had become "the drunk-
en Helot of literature." In the popular mind there has
been little change in Machiavelli's reputation, and the
words "Machiavellian" and "Machiavellianism" still
carry these implications in ordinary language today.

Although Shakespeare's contemporary, Francis Bacon,
noted without disapproval that Machiavelli dealt with
men as they are, not as they ought to be, nowhere in
the world of criticism and scholarship was there to be
for a century and a half any serious attempt to rehabili-
tate Machiavelli's reputation.

IV

THE ESTIMATE of Machiavelli in the learned world did
not differ substantially from the popular conception.
That is why no change in the cultural history of Western Europe is more striking than the reestimate which

historians and political scientists are in process of making or have already made of Machiavelli's once notorious and now famous work.

In his *History of Political Theories* W. H. Dunning tells us that Machiavelli's work is as completely dissevered from the older accepted systems of political theory as the discovery of America by his contemporary Columbus is dissevered from the older accepted systems of geography. We might add that for nearly three centuries it will remain dissevered from the main currents of modern political thought. Machiavelli will begin to impinge upon these modern currents in the late eighteenth century, and in some of their phases at least will come near dominating them in the nineteenth and twentieth centuries.

Aristotle is often classified as a realist, and his treatise on *Politics* was to influence greatly the pre-Machiavellian trend of thought. Perhaps nothing can serve better to set forth the difference in spirit between the older tradition and Machiavelli than to remind the reader of Aristotle's opening sentence and have him compare it with the opening of *The Prince*. It reads:

Seeing that every state is a sort of association and every association is formed for the attainment of some Good —for some presumed Good is the end of all action— it is evident that, as some Good is the object of all associations, so in the highest degree is the supreme Good the object of that association which is supreme and embraces all the rest, in other words, of the State or political association.

A brief sample chapter in Aristotle can be summarized as follows:

Three qualifications are requisite in the holders of the supreme offices of the State:

1.) loyalty to the polity
2.) capacity for their offices
3.) virtue and justice in the sense appropriate to the polity.

Then, in discussing how a polity may best be preserved, he adds that the best of all preservatives is the education of the citizens in the spirit of the polity: "Without this education the wisest laws are futile."

Machiavelli is not concerned with the education of the citizens. They are regarded as inert. The state is no longer an instrument for achieving the good life. It has become a dynamic, amoral entity, a force. Many contemporary students of Machiavelli, like Leonardo Olschki in *Machiavelli the Scientist,* will point out that he is more scientific than Aristotle or any other of his predecessors, and that this is what constitutes Machiavelli's break with tradition. There is much truth in this contention. As Olschki puts it, "The state is in Machiavelli's mind a merely theoretical reality, an abstract principle whose practical realization is represented by principalities or republics." It is only a slight exaggeration to say that the role of the prince is to direct this force according to principles which in essence are very much like those by which the scientist directs the course of a guided missile. There is no inherent purpose in the state. Any direction it may receive must be imposed upon it by the ruler.

It was not, however, in the first instance, the recognition of this "scientific" quality of Machiavelli's work that accounted for the renewed interest in Machiavelli. This arose from a quite different consideration which will not be clearly evident to the reader until he reaches the very last chapter of *The Prince.* The "exhortation to liberate Italy from the barbarians" with its fervent hope that "some individual might be appointed by God for her redemption" is the most eloquent passage in Machiavelli's work. Its dithyrambic quality stands out so sharply against the purely intellectual, almost algebraic presentation of the rest of *The Prince* that until recently it was often regarded by scholars as a later appendage and not an integral part of the work. In spite of the seeming inconsistency, there is nothing to support the contention that it was added later. The explanation lies in the fact that Machiavelli was both scientific and an ardent patriot, and it was the nationalism that first brought him back into favor.

Earlier political theory had paid relatively little attention to the rights of the nation as such. France and England, for instance, even in Machiavelli's own time, had made much greater progress than Italy toward national unity. But the notion of sovereignty, which was much discussed in political theory, was still tied up with notions of hereditary monarchy. The recognized powers of the hereditary prince were such that it was still possible even for the last of the Hohenzollerns to hold that he was king by divine right, and we still find even on English coins the legend, *Dei Gratia Rex*, long after the English had accepted a Hanoverian as their king. The powers of hereditary princes during the Wars of Religion after Machiavelli's time were still so strongly established that the prince's right to determine the religion his subjects were to follow was widely recognized. In the seventeenth and eighteenth centuries the central political problem which these countries were called upon to solve was one in which Machiavelli's prince had little interest. The fundamental law of monarchies like the English and the French recognized the authority of the monarch and the right to succession. The immediate problem they were concerned with had little to do with nation states as such but was cardinal to the shaping of modern democracies, even our own. It was this: What rights have subjects, when the powers of a properly constituted monarch are improperly executed? This was the issue and the most pressing problem in political theory in the English, the French, and the American revolutions. This problem was to be settled by an appeal to principles of natural law that were deeply rooted both in the practice and the theory of Roman law but in which Machiavelli's prince showed no interest. Even a cursory rereading of our Declaration of Independence with its indictment of the King of England will indicate that in 1776 we were not insisting on the rights of nationality. We did not justify our founding a new state because of our Americanism, but because our fundamental human rights to life, liberty, and the pursuit of happiness had been violated by the King of England whose subjects we had previously

been. The nationalistic considerations which were to
bring Machiavelli so prominently into nineteenth-century
thinking were, however, already developing.

v

EVER SINCE the Renaissance, of which, oddly enough,
Machiavelli was otherwise so representative a member,
it had been quite generally recognized by historians,
and political scientists as well, that Western European
civilization had its roots in antiquity, that it was a con-
tinuous development, with something like what in medicine is called a remission during the "Dark Ages."
Eighteenth-century scholars particularly were to bring a
line of inquiry which eventually would lead to other
conclusions and tend to disrupt the earlier conscious-
ness of antiquity. By students of literature this is generally called the Romantic Revolt. In one of its phases it
was deeply interested in the mediaeval period as such
and led to a greatly heightened interest in mediaeval
and folk poetry. This movement was to be particularly
pronounced in Germany, which had not yet made any
progress toward national unity. Germany had, of course,
been less Romanized than Western Europe and it is not
surprising that Germany should have been more inclined
to seek for the origins of her culture in her own mediaeval folk poetry, customs, and institutions. It was this
new current of thought which was to result in what was
called in Hitler's time the Revolt Against the West, which
meant the revolt against the Graeco-Roman tradition.
This glorification of the Folk had much to do with
emphasizing, perhaps overemphasizing, national origins
and nationalism in general. The Folk began to be con-
ceived as a kind of mystic entity or person, presumably
united by ties of blood. As a mystic entity and a legal
person, sovereign rights were inherent in it, and in it
only. Machiavelli, of course, had no such notion of an
Italian Folk. Italians to him were the direct descendants
of the Romans. To him the Italians, above all other
peoples, deserved to have a nation state of their own, and

the increasing momentum to nationalize institutions and to create nation states in the rest of Europe did bring his own nationalism again into the foreground and bring this trend in his thinking back into the main current of the nineteenth century.

VI

EARLY in the nineteenth century Hegel's philosophy was to see in the state the instrument through which God works his will upon or, perhaps rather, through history. This tended to place the forces which shape man's world beyond human control. Both of these conceptions, that of the nation as a mystic entity rooted in the Folk, and Hegel's notion of the state as a divinely ordained force and ultimate power in shaping civilization were steadily to gather momentum and to merge into the notion of the nation state. This paved the way for a far more favorable attitude toward the nationalistic ideas of *The Prince*. The ban that had been laid upon Machiavelli was to be lifted. In Italy the achievement of national unity of which he was so clearly the prophet would make him a hero. Italians made of the 400th anniversary of his birth in 1869 a national celebration, and the plaque which his native city Florence placed over his tomb reads: *Tanto Nomini Nullum par Elogium* (For so great a name no praise is adequate).

Lay readers of recent discussions of *The Prince* by political scientists are inclined to draw an erroneous conclusion. They know that Hitler, Mussolini, and Stalin have pursued courses of action, like the "purge," which are in accordance with maxims prescribed by Machiavelli. When they see that these recent studies of *The Prince* are generally favorable to Machiavelli's central conceptions they conclude that political scientists have "gone fascist." At the risk of seeming to digress for a moment a word of explanation is here necessary.

Political leaders of all types ever since Machiavelli's time have always found much to their purpose in *The Prince*. It should not surprise us, however, to find that in the earlier nineteenth century German historians should have become particularly interested in Machiavelli. Germany's central political problem, like Italy's, was that of achieving national unity. At that time Ranke, usually regarded as the ablest German historian and the founder of modern historical method, was still troubled occasionally. There is a touch of apology in his statement that Machiavelli, recognizing the desperate disease of Italy, had "the courage to prescribe poison." This would bring at least a few of Machiavelli's deadliest prescriptions under the heading of what we now call "mercy killings." But Ranke holds consistently that Machiavelli has been much maligned by people who did not understand him and that he was "an author of the highest desert and one who was in no sense an evil man." Certainly one of Germany's ablest historians in the twentieth century is Friedrich Meinecke. Probably no earlier writer has more deeply influenced him than Machiavelli, and Meinecke is the author of the consistently favorable and indeed eulogistic study of *The Prince* which serves as introduction to the standard modern German translation. The question of date is here highly important. Ranke's view of history was influenced by the thinking and events of the nineteenth century. Meinecke's more pessimistic outlook was shaped in the twentieth century, and his study of *The Prince* was written in the confused period after World War I. Yet Meinecke himself showed high courage in refusing to accept Hitler's pretensions to be the Führer of the German people, and refused to submit when Hitler sought to establish thought control in the German universities. In contemporary Italy, likewise, one of the most courageous opponents of Mussolini was Count Carlo Sforza. Yet Sforza is also the author of a recent volume on the *Living Thoughts of Machiavelli* which emphasizes the enduring validity of much of Machiavelli's thinking.

In France, England, and America scholarly opinion was slower to shift toward a more favorable estimate of Machiavelli. Few historians in England have been more consistently concerned about the maintenance of civil liberties than Lord Acton, and his famous statement about the corruptive influence of power is too well known to need repetition. Yet it was Acton who in the last decade of the nineteenth century wrote the generally favorable introduction to L. A. Burd's edition and study of *The Prince*. Scholarly interest in Machiavelli in our own country began after World War I and its most important contributions have been made during the past decade. To avoid possible misunderstanding it must therefore be emphasized that if American students of political theory have become more favorably disposed toward Machiavelli it is not because they have "gone fascist" but because they are attempting to go scientific. It may be that there is an error involved in this and that it has been carried too far. We must also consider in a moment how this trend arose. But to keep our consideration of Machiavelli in perspective it is necessary to remind ourselves that if there is any error involved, it is intellectual error, and that it is one of the fundamental tenets of American democracy that intellectual error is innocent.

VII

IN ONE SENSE, at least, it is unfortunate that the study of politics should so generally be called political science. It can never be a science in the same sense that physics is a science, based on experimentation and measurement. In every political decision there must always remain a certain element of calculated risk. Modern scholars who are inclined to accept Machiavelli's guided missile theory of the relation between the state and the prince are accepting only a loose analogy between politics and physics. In the natural sciences, an experiment is the scientist's way of asking nature a question. That is what Franklin was doing when he flew his kite into the thunderstorm. He asked whether or not lightning was an electrical phenomenon. It was nature and not Franklin that gave the answer. Into such scientific answers the "personal equation" does not enter. The political scientist has no such rigorous method at his disposal. The best he can do is to study the motivation of princes in concrete situations without any preconceived ideas. Machiavelli held that,

of such preconceived ideas which prevent arriving at the
truth, the most serious is the idea that princes follow, or
should follow, the same moral code that governs the conduct of private individuals. Machiavelli therefore completely divorced the study of politics from the study of
ethics. They have nothing in commion. But here we
quickly run into one of several psychological contradic-
tions into which Machiavelli's rigorous realism leads him.
He recommends to the prince that he use hypocrisy,
whenever expedient, to gain power. This cannot be effective in the long run, since the prince's important relations are with other princes. It takes no idealism to tell
us this. The Frenchman La Rochefoucauld is not usually
rated as an idealist, yet in a famous maxim he tells us
that "hypocrisy is the tribute which vice pays to virtue."
By this he means that hypocrisy works only because the
majority of men are not hypocrites and are therefore not
suspicious. When all princes practice deceit it soon fails
to get results for any of them. This is what happened to
Machiavelli's hero, Cesare Borgia. He had acquired con-
siderable power through the use of force and fraud. He
lost it when other princes successfully used the same
method against him. When in their desire to become
scientific, political theorists and historians like Meinecke
create a "Political Man" on the model of Machiavelli's
prince, he is likely to become for the purposes of inter-
preting human history as misleading an abstraction as the
"Economic Man" postulated by a school of economists
actuated by the same desire to be scientific. This desire
is the quite natural reaction to the unwarranted assump-
tions and soft thinking with which students of politics
as well as political leaders and citizens generally entered
the twentieth century.

VIII

NINETEENTH-CENTURY thinking was excessively optimistic.
That was because nearly all of us, including historians,
had come to believe that progress was the underlying
law of civilization. There might be brief halts or even

temporary reverses, but there was something in the nature of the world and in the nature of man that made civilization proceed in a humanly desirable direction. Nineteenth-century thinking was also excessively nationalistic and nearly all history was written in nationalistic terms. In dealing with the nation states historians traced them from their crude beginnings in the barbaric clans of the Folk to their greatness, and the nation came to be regarded as the predestined instrument of progress. In dealing with other peoples who had not yet achieved national unity, it was assumed that the course of progress had somehow been delayed (usually by selfish local potentates) but that they would soon, and inevitably, likewise achieve nationhood. With the unification of Italy and Germany it was very generally assumed that humanity was now ready to take an immense step forward. This generally optimistic and nationalistic trend of thought continued through World War I. How generally we believed that the nation was an inherently beneficent entity is nowhere more clearly indicated than in the very general acceptance without qualifications of the principle of the "self-determination of nationality." Like the king in an earlier theory of politics, it was assumed that the nation could do no wrong. The persecution of minorities within self-determined nations, the rise of national fascism, and the failure, within twenty years, of a League of Nations, have given us all, including historians and political scientists, a rude awakening. The unwelcome conclusion that the nation as such was not a benevolent entity received further confirmation from another development that had occurred after World War I. Karl Marx had made a new interpretation of history about 1850. He retained much of Hegel's idea that the forces of history are not humanly directed but operate autonomously, indeed automatically. He did eliminate God as a useless hypothesis, and his interpretation of history was antinationalistic. Though Marx's theories were widely discussed, they assumed first-rate political importance only after the Russian Soviets accepted them and gave them a nationalistic core and center. This definitely put an end

to nineteenth-century thinking. The phrase so frequently
and so favorably used in the nineteenth century, the
"family of nations," is no longer heard. If there is any
such family, it is now a very unhappy family. Anyone
who will take the pains to consult maps of Europe and
Asia as of 1910, or 1930, and 1950, cannot help but be
struck by the continual shifting of boundaries, the appearance and disappearance of states, and would have to
conclude that in our much more crowded and closely-
packed world, the nation state of the twentieth century
is in as unstable and as chaotic a condition as were the
city states of Italy in Machiavelli's day.

IX

IT IS NOT difficult to understand why, in the present chaos
of nation states so like that of Machiavelli's city states,
there should have been a revival of interest in Machiavelli's ideas.

Many of his twentieth-century critics hold that Machiavelli was the first modern man. In two respects he
appears to be so. On the negative side, Machiavelli never
believed in progress and many modern men have ceased
to believe in it. On the positive side, Machiavelli believed
in the nation: he also believed in scientific method, at
least to the point of getting rid of superannuated precon-
ceptions. Superficially, at least, our problems are similar
to his. Twentieth-century man wants peace and "security"
for his state and for himself. Machiavelli was not interested in peace and did not believe it was necessary. But
wars in his day were milk and water affairs as compared
to ours. If they had not been, the great artistic and
architectural monuments of Rome, Florence, and Venice
would never have survived. He did want security for his
city and he believed this could be achieved by a prince
who would compel such city states to merge into a nation
state.

It is evident in Machiavelli's *Discourses on Livy* that
to him this nation state of Italy was to be the inheritor
of the greatness of the Roman Republic. It is evident in

all of his works that he regarded Italians as superior to
other breeds of men. The depredations of the Spaniards
and French in Italy were made possible only by their
superior political organization. Once Italy had achieved
such statehood, he believed that with her more advanta-
geous geographical position on the Mediterranean, on
her *mare nostrum,* she could again establish her domination over the civilized world. Since Rome had succeeded
in doing this, the descendants of the Romans with a
similarly effective organization, with favorable fortune,
and the same manifestation of Roman *virtu* could enter-
tain the hope of doing so again. It is Machiavelli's deeply
humiliating sense of how are the mighty fallen that ex-
plains that impassioned eloquence of his last chapter
which has so often puzzled his commentators. Nineteenth-
century historians were unanimous in favoring Italy in
her heroic struggle for unification. They believed that
once she had achieved it she would happily and content-
edly assume her predestined place in the family of nations.

It was generally overlooked, and indeed still is by many
commentators, that there is perhaps unfortunately nothing to indicate that Machiavelli would have altered his
advice to the prince once Italy had become a nation.
The real or supposedly scientific quality of *The Prince*
makes its advice for the conduct of the ruler generally
applicable. In this respect, Mussolini was far more truly
Machiavelli's disciple than Mazzini who, though he
worked for Italian unification, bitterly opposed his other
ideas. To Machiavelli the state, the nation state as well
as any other, remains a force and its essence is to be
dynamic and aggressive. One of our ablest American students of political science, writing shortly before World
War I, drew the conclusion that nationalism is proving
to be "only a temporary and transitional phase of the
trend toward expansion." Until we recognize this more
fully we can understand neither Machiavelli nor the in-
ternational problems of our time.

It is, as we have seen, from Machiavelli's scientific
concept of the state as force that he derives the rule of

conduct which he recommends to the prince. A force as such, a bullet or a bomb, has no ethical principles, and we have seen that those of the prince are not binding but are on a take-it-or-leave-it basis. We know that the condition in which a state finds itself alters the code even of the citizen of a democracy. When his country is at war, he is no longer bound to respect the sanctity of life and to obey the commandment *thou shalt not kill.* When his country is in danger it becomes his duty to defend it. Since the ruler is more directly responsible for the safety of the state than the average citizen, his code in time of war would be more seriously affected. What shocked earlier readers of *The Prince* and still shocks some of them is that what Ranke called the poison which Machiavelli prescribed can be used by the prince indiscriminately both against fellow citizens who, for some reason, are unwilling to accept his rule, and against external enemies. There are passages in *The Prince* in which it seems that Machiavelli's criterion of the validity of law is also derived from his concept of force. So for instance:

> As there cannot be good laws where the state is not well armed, it follows that where they are all armed they have good laws. I shall leave the laws out of the discussion and speak of the arms.

In the nineteenth century, when the later nation states like Germany and Italy emerged, the nation was not regarded primarily as a force but as a benevolent guardian of the sovereign rights of its people. These sovereign rights which each nation enjoyed nevertheless made the larger world in which they lived a lawless world. Nineteenth-century man, with his faith in progress and the nation, was inclined to regard this world of the nation states as a kind of utopia at the end of history, somewhat as the Marxist regards his utopia of the eventual classless society. If there was no other law over the sovereign nation, there did remain what has sometimes been called the first law of nature, self-preservation. Many crimes were committed in its name. No nation could afford to see its neighbors become too strong and various forms of imperialism, colonialism, and even "preventive wars" were undertaken in the name of the national interest or of manifest destiny. Such actions were justified as necessary for reasons of state, and in the absence of any other principle, this became in fact the only law. On this showing Machiavelli would have had the right to conclude that the core of the state was power. In regarding the state as a dynamic expansive force, Machiavelli was closer to reality and *Realpolitik* than much nineteenth- and early twentieth-century thinking, and in this respect is modern.

x

IN ANOTHER respect we must repeat that Machiavelli was not modern, and remained an Italian humanist of the Renaissance. He had no sense for what we call historical evolution. He found his ideals in Rome. For him the Roman Republic marked the high point in human achievement and it is plain throughout *The Discourses* that to him the Roman Republic itself was the most highly perfected form of government that man had devised. He so greatly admires its institutions that one of the ablest contemporary French students of Machiavelli, Renaudet, concludes that if Machiavelli had been called upon to devise the constitution for a modern state it would certainly have included consuls, a senate, and tribunes, and would have repeated in substance and in terminology Roman ideas. It would have been far more like the Constitution devised after the French Revolution by the Jacobins, who were also great admirers of the Romans, than like that which the American colonists in pain and travail devised to meet the needs of a people who after seven years of revolution found themselves called upon to create something approaching an ideal form of government for free men. Upon our form of government and what we call Jeffersonian democracy, it can be said that he had no influence whatever. A re-reading of much of Jefferson and a scanning of the indices to all of his published work have failed to disclose a single reference to Machiavelli.

Nowhere in *The Prince* is there any limit placed upon
the power of the state, and it was this problem of limiting state power that concerned Jefferson.

The origins of the doctrine of the unalienable rights
of man are too well known to need more than passing
reference here. Oddly enough the theory arose in the
decline of the Greek city states. Greek thinkers had earlier reached the conclusion that the world of nature was
a cosmos, a world of laws discoverable by the human
reason. As a result of the conquest of much of the East
by Alexander the Great, there were far more contacts
between their citizens and those of other states. The
Stoics became deeply conscious that men lived in One
World, that they were all citizens of one great city which
they called cosmopolis. This world of man, too, has its
laws, and they too must be recognized if man is to realize
his human potential.

This could be dismissed as empty theorizing. But oddly
enough at about the same time the more practical Romans were confronted with a similar problem. Members
of non-Roman peoples or tribes were beginning to flock
to Rome to pursue commerce or enjoy her greater security. As non-citizens they as yet had no legal rights or
status. Roman magistrates sought to discover a common
denominator for the laws of all peoples and, so they
believed, found it in what they called the law of nations,
which they concluded must be the fundamental law. This
was the basis of those laws of nature and of nature's God
to which Jefferson appealed in our Declaration of Independence, and was to provide the basis of our modern
conceptions of human rights and of equity. All this entered into the basic concepts of Roman jurisprudence
which was to affect so deeply European civilization, and
our own. The contemporary German school of historians
represented by Machiavelli's great admirer Meinecke
condemns all those who indulge in what he calls the
natural right type of thinking. It is strange to find that
Machiavelli, as the great admirer of Rome, should have
been very little concerned with Roman jurisprudence,
perhaps her greatest single contribution to civilization.

THAT MAN has survived at all in spite of his physical inferiority to lions, for instance, is not the result of the fraud or trickery of a few individuals. Though there always have been, and always will be, many evil men, man owes his survival through nearly half a million years, and the civilizations he has shaped in the last six thousand, to something inherent in his nature. That is why we must regard civilization as natural to man. That is why Aristotle was right when he held that man was a political or social animal. The state is not something outside of our human world. The particular form of the state under which men live is not imposed by either God or the devil. To some degree, at least, it is man's creation and like other human creations subject to his revision. So too the Stoics were right when they believed, as we have seen, that all men lived in a cosmopolis, a world of man which is a different world, a potentially larger world than that of lions or foxes. It is possible for the less human and the less humane among men to live quite like beasts of prey and to seek only their own. But such drives for selfish power are possible because the many believe in their inherent need for cooperation and human fellowship. Since man is creatively intelligent there are bound to be differences and clashes, even disastrous and fatal clashes about the many possible forms which the fellowship of the tribe, or the city, or the nation, or the world of men shall take. But some sense of the common interest, of a tie that binds, does remain. That is why modern men are still interested in ancient cities and how men lived in them. The leader will often be foiled by the perverseness and recalcitrance of his generation, but so far as he is intelligent, he knows that his social nature and need involves a code of conduct which is, of course, a moral code, and that to some degree each should strive for the welfare of all. Common men know this so well that they do not place Cesare Borgia and Ivan the Terrible on the same plane with St. Louis of France or George Washington. Though he does not reveal it in *The Prince,* this sense of man's nature and need is not strange to Machiavelli. In his *Discourses on Livy* he bids the reader

> *note how much more praise those Emperors merited who, after Rome became an empire, conformed to the laws like good princes, than those who took the opposite course; and he will see that Titus, Nerva, Trajan, Hadrian, Antoninus, and Marcus Aurelius did not require the Praetorians nor the multitudinous legions to defend them, because they were protected by their own good conduct, the good will of the people, and by the love of the Senate.*

The sense that we live in a cosmos, that there is uniformity, and that there are laws of nature, has been so strongly reinforced by the steady advance of science, that few now are tempted to deny it. This does not exclude possible catastrophe and waste. The faults which cause the earthquake are a consequence of the working of nature's laws as much as the return of spring or the blossoming of the rose, and the canker will kill many a bud. So in human affairs and in man's cosmopolis there will be desperate and deadly revolutions and many foiled lives.

Machiavelli had spent thirteen years in earnest striving to improve the lot of his country, and learned much that is revealing and valid. His reward was exile. It is idle to deny that *The Prince* is a bitter book. Its bitterness is the result of his failure in his time. The modern reader cannot afford to allow this to blind him to what it contains which is still valid for our own day.

THE PRINCE

Niccolò Machiavelli
To
Lorenzo The Magnificent
Son of Piero Di Medici

IT IS CUSTOMARY for those who wish to gain the favour of a prince to endeavour to do so by offering him gifts of those things which they hold most precious, or in which they know him to take especial delight. In this way princes are often presented with horses, arms, cloth of gold, gems, and such-like ornaments worthy of their grandeur. In my desire, however, to offer to Your Highness some humble testimony of my devotion, I have been unable to find among my possessions anything which I hold so dear or esteem so highly as that knowledge of the deeds of great men which I have acquired through a long experience of modern events and a constant study of the past.

With the utmost diligence I have long pondered and scrutinised the actions of the great, and now I offer the results to Your Highness within the compass of a small volume: and although I deem this work unworthy of Your Highness's acceptance, yet my confidence in your humanity assures me that you will receive it with favour, knowing that it is not in my power to offer you a greater gift than that of enabling you to understand in a very short time all those things which I have learnt at the cost of privation and danger in the course of many years. I have not sought to adorn my work with long phrases or high-sounding words or any of those superficial attractions and ornaments with which many writers seek to embellish their material, as I desire no honour for my work but such as the novelty and gravity of its subject may justly deserve. Nor will it, I trust, be deemed presumptuous on the part of a man of humble and obscure condition to attempt to discuss and direct the government of princes; for in the same way that landscape painters station themselves in the valleys in order to draw mountains or high ground, and ascend an eminence in order to get a good view of the plains, so it is necessary to be a prince to know thoroughly the nature of the people, and one of the populace to know the nature of princes.

May I trust, therefore, that Your Highness will accept this little gift in the spirit in which it is offered; and if Your Highness will deign to peruse it, you will recognise in it my ardent desire that you may attain to that grandeur which fortune and your own merits presage for you.

And should Your Highness gaze down from the summit of your lofty position towards this humble spot, you will recognise the great and unmerited sufferings inflicted on me by a cruel fate.

1

The Various Kinds of Government and the Ways by Which They Are Established

ALL STATES and dominions which hold or have held sway over mankind are either republics or monarchies. Monarchies are either hereditary in which the rulers have been for many years of the same family, or else they are of recent foundation. The newly founded ones are either entirely new, as was Milan to Francesco Sforza, or else they are, as it were, new members grafted on to the hereditary possessions of the prince that annexes them, as is the kingdom of Naples to the King of Spain. The dominions thus acquired have either been previously accustomed to the rule of another prince, or else have been free states, and they are annexed either by force of arms of the prince himself, or of others, or else fall to him by good fortune or special ability.

2

Of Hereditary Monarchies

I WILL NOT here speak of republics, having already treated of them fully in another place. I will deal only with monarchies, and will discuss how the various kinds described above can be governed and maintained. In the first place, the difficulty of maintaining hereditary states accustomed to a reigning family is far less than in new monarchies; for it is sufficient not to transgress ancestral usages, and to adapt one's self to unforeseen circumstances; in this way such a prince, if of ordinary assiduity, will always be able to maintain his position, unless some very exceptional and excessive force deprives him of it; and even if he be thus deprived, on the slightest mischance happening to the new occupier, he will be able to regain it.

We have in Italy the example of the Duke of Ferrara, who was able to withstand the assaults of the Venetians in 1484 and of Pope Julius in 1510, for no other reason than because of the antiquity of his family in that dominion. In as much as the legitimate prince has less cause and less necessity to give offence, it is only natural that he should be more loved; and, if no extraordinary vices make him hated, it is only reasonable for his subjects to be naturally attached to him, the memories and causes of innovations being forgotten in the long period over which his rule has extended; whereas one change always leaves the way prepared for the introduction of another.

3

Of Mixed Monarchies

BUT IT IS in the new monarchy that difficulties really exist. First, if it is not entirely new, but a member as it were of a mixed state, its disorders spring at first from a natural difficulty which exists in all new dominions, because men change masters willingly, hoping to better themselves; and this belief makes them take arms against their rulers, in which they are deceived, as experience later proves that they have gone from bad to worse. This is the result of another very natural cause, which is the inevitable harm inflicted on those over whom the prince obtains dominion, both by his soldiers and by an infinite number of other injuries caused by his occupation.

Thus you find enemies in all those whom you have injured by occupying that dominion, and you cannot maintain the friendship of those who have helped you to obtain this possession, as you will not be able to fulfil their expectations, nor can you use strong measures with them, being under an obligation to them; for which reason, however strong your armies may be, you will always need the favour of the inhabitants to take possession of a province. It was from these causes that Louis XII of France, though able to occupy Milan without trouble, immediately lost it, and the forces of Ludovico alone were sufficient to take it from him the first time, for the inhabitants who had willingly opened their gates to him, finding themselves deluded in the hopes they had cherished and not obtaining those benefits they had anticipated, could not bear the vexatious rule of their new prince.

It is indeed true that, after reconquering rebel territories they are not so easily lost again, for the ruler is now, by the fact of the rebellion, less averse to secure his position by punishing offenders, unmasking suspects, and strengthening himself in weak places. So that although the mere appearance of such a person as Duke Ludovico on the frontier was sufficient to cause France to lose Milan the first time, to make her lose her grip of it the second time was only possible when all the world was against her, and after her armies had been defeated and driven out of Italy; which was the result of the causes above mentioned. Nevertheless it was taken from her both the first and the second time. The general causes of the first loss have been already discussed; it remains now to be seen what were the causes of the second loss and by what means France could have avoided it, or what measures might have been taken by another ruler in that position which were not taken by the King of France. Be it observed, therefore, that those states which on annexation are united to a previously existing state may or may not be of the same nationality and language. If they are, it is very easy to hold them, especially if they are not accustomed to freedom; and to possess them securely it suffices that the family of the princes which formerly governed them be extinct. For the rest, their old condition not being disturbed, and there being no dissimilarity of customs, the people settle down quietly under their new rulers, as is seen in the case of Burgundy, Brittany, Gascony, and Normandy, which have been so long united to France; and although there may be some slight differences of language, the customs of the people are nevertheless similar, and they can get along well together. Whoever obtains possession of such territories and wishes to retain them must bear in mind two things: the one, that the blood of their old rulers be extinct; the other, to make no alteration either in their laws or in their taxes; in this way they will in a very short space of time become united with their old possessions and form one state.

But when dominions are acquired in a province differing in language, laws and customs, the difficulties to be overcome are great, and it requires good fortune as well as great industry to retain them; one of the best and most certain means of doing so would be for the new ruler to take up his residence there. This would render possession more secure and durable, and it is what the Turk has done in Greece. In spite of all the other measures taken by him to hold that state, it would not have been possible to retain it had he not gone to live there. Being on the spot, disorders can be seen as they arise and can quickly be remedied, but living at a distance, they are only heard of when they get beyond remedy. Besides which, the province is not despoiled by your officials, the subjects being able to obtain satisfaction by direct recourse to their prince; and wishing to be loyal they have more reason to love him, and should they be otherwise inclined they will have greater cause to fear him. Any external Power who wishes to assail that state will be less disposed to do so; so that as long as he resides there he will be very hard to dispossess.

The other and better remedy is to plant colonies in one or two of those places which form as it were the keys of the land, for it is necessary either to do this or to maintain a large force of armed men. The colonies will cost the prince little; with little or no expense on his part, he can send and maintain them; he only injures those whose lands and houses are taken to give to the new inhabitants, and these form but a small proportion of the state, and those who are injured, remaining poor and scattered, can never do any harm to him, and all the others are, on the one hand, not injured and therefore easily pacified; and, on the other, are fearful of offending lest they should be treated like those who have been dispossessed. To conclude, these colonies cost nothing, are more faithful, and give less offence; and the injured parties being poor and scattered are unable to do mischief, as I have shown. For it must be noted, that men must either be caressed or else annihilated; they will revenge themselves for small injuries, but cannot do so for great ones; the injury therefore that we do to a man must be such that we need not fear his vengeance. But by maintaining a garrison instead of colonists, one will spend much more, and consume all the revenues of that state in guarding it, so that the acquisition will result in a loss, besides giving much greater offence, since it injures every one in that state with the quartering of the army on it; which being an inconvenience felt by all, every one becomes an enemy, and these are enemies which can do mischief, as, though beaten, they remain in their own homes. In every way, therefore, a garrison is as useless as colonies are useful.

Further, the ruler of a foreign province as described, should make himself the leader and defender of his less powerful neighbours, and endeavour to weaken the stronger ones, and take care that they are not invaded by some foreigner not less powerful than himself. And it will be always the case that he will be invited to intervene at the request of those who are discontented either through ambition or fear, as was seen when the Ætolians invited the Romans into Greece; and in whatever province they entered, it was always at the request of the inhabitants. And the rule is that when a powerful foreigner enters a province, all the less powerful inhabitants become his adherents, moved by the envy they bear to those ruling over them; so much so that with regard to these minor potentates he has no trouble whatever in winning them over, for they willingly join forces with the state that he has acquired. He has merely to be careful that they do not assume too much power and authority, and he can easily with his own forces and their favour put down those that are powerful and remain in everything arbiter of that province. And he who does not govern well in this way will soon lose what he has acquired, and while he holds it will meet with infinite difficulty and trouble.

The Romans in the provinces they took, always followed this policy; they established colonies, inveigled the less powerful without increasing their strength, put down the most powerful and did not allow foreign rulers to obtain influence in them. I will adduce the province of Greece as a sole example. They made friends with the Achæans and the Ætolians, the kingdom of Macedonia was cast down, and Antiochus driven out, nor did they allow the merits of the Achæans or the Ætolians to gain them any increase of territory, nor did the persuasions of Philip induce them to befriend him without reducing his influence, nor could the power of Antiochus make them consent to allow him to hold any state in that province.

For the Romans did in these cases what all wise princes should do, who consider not only present but also future discords and diligently guard against them; for being foreseen they can easily be remedied, but if one waits till they are at hand, the medicine is no longer in time as the malady has become incurable; it happening with this as with those hectic fevers, as doctors say, which at their beginning are easy to cure but difficult to recognise, but in course of time when they have not at first been recognised and treated, become easy to recognise and difficult to cure. Thus it happens in matters of state; for knowing afar off (which it is only given to a prudent man to do) the evils that are brewing, they are easily cured. But when, for want of such knowledge, they are allowed to grow so that every one can recognise them, there is no longer any remedy to be found. Therefore, the Romans, observing disorders while yet remote, were always able to find a remedy, and never allowed them to increase in order to avoid a war; for they knew that war is not to be avoided, and can be deferred only to the advantage of the other side; they therefore declared war against Philip and Antiochus in Greece, so as not to have to fight them in Italy, though they might at the time have avoided either; this they did not choose to do, never caring to do that which is now every day to be heard in the mouths of our wise men, namely to enjoy the advantages of delay, but preferring to trust their own virtue and prudence; for time brings with it all things, and may produce indifferently either good or evil.

But let us return to France and examine whether she did any of these things; and I will speak not of Charles, but of Louis as the one whose proceedings can be better seen, as he held possession in Italy for a longer time; you will then see that he did the opposite of all those things which must be done to keep possession of a foreign state. King Louis was called into Italy by the ambition of the Venetians, who wished by his coming to gain half of Lombardy. I will not blame the king for coming nor for the part he took, because wishing to plant his foot in Italy, and not having friends in the country, on the contrary the conduct of King Charles having caused all doors to be closed to him, he was forced to accept what friendships he could find, and his schemes would have speedily been successful if he had made no mistakes in his other proceedings.

The king then, having acquired Lombardy, immediately won back the reputation lost by Charles. Genoa yielded, the Florentines became his friends, the Marquis of Mantua, the Dukes of Ferrara and Bentivogli, the Lady of Forlì, the Lords of Faenza, Pesaro, Rimini, Camerino, and Piombino, the inhabitants of Lucca, of Pisa, and of Siena, all approached him with offers of friendship. The Venetians might then have seen the effects of their temerity, how to gain a few cities in Lombardy they had made the king ruler over two-thirds of Italy.

Consider how little difficulty the king would have had in maintaining his reputation in Italy if he had observed the aforesaid rules, and kept a firm and sure hold over all those friends of his, who being many in number and weak, and fearful, one of the Church, another of the Venetians, were always obliged to hold fast to him, and by whose aid he could easily make sure of any who were still great. But he was hardly in Milan before he did exactly the opposite, by giving aid to Pope Alexander to occupy the Romagna. Nor did he perceive that, in taking this course, he weakened himself, by casting off his friends and those who had fled to his protection, and strengthened the Church by adding further temporal powers to the spiritual power, which gives it such authority. And having made the first mistake, he was obliged to follow it up, whilst, to put a stop to the ambition of Alexander and prevent him becoming ruler of Tuscany, he was forced to come to Italy. And not content with having increased the power of the Church and lost his

friends, he now coveting the kingdom of Naples, divided
it with the king of Spain; and where he alone was the
arbiter of Italy, he now brought in a companion, so that
the ambitious of that province who were dissatisfied with
him might have some one else to appeal to; and where
he might have left in that kingdom a king tributary to
himself, he dispossessed him in order to bring in another
who was capable of driving him out.

The desire to acquire possessions is a very natural and
ordinary thing, and when those men do it who can do
so successfully, they are always praised and not blamed,
but when they cannot and yet want to do so at all costs,
they make a mistake deserving of great blame. If France,
therefore, with her own forces could have taken Naples,
she ought to have done so; if she could not, she ought
not to have shared it. And if the partition of Lombardy
with the Venetians is to be excused, as having been the
means of allowing the French king to set foot in Italy,
this other partition deserves blame, not having the excuse
of necessity.

Louis had thus made these five mistakes: he had
crushed the smaller Powers, increased the power in Italy
of one potentate, brought into the land a very powerful
foreigner, he had not come to live there himself, nor had
he established any colonies. Still these mistakes, if he had
lived, might not have injured him, had he not made the
sixth, that of taking the state from the Venetians; for, if
he had not strengthened the Church and brought the
Spaniards into Italy, it would have been right and
necessary to humble them; having once taken those measures, he ought never to have consented to their ruin; because, had the Venetians been strong, it would have kept
the others from making attempts on Lombardy, partly
because the Venetians would not have consented to any
measures by which they did not get it for themselves, and
partly because the others would not have wanted to take
it from France to give it to Venice, and would not have
had the courage to attack both.

If any one urges that King Louis yielded Romagna
to Alexander and the Kingdom of Naples to Spain in

order to avoid war, I reply with the reasons already given, that one ought never to allow a disorder to take place in order to avoid war, for war is not thereby avoided, but only deferred to your disadvantage. And if others allege the promise given by the king to the pope to undertake that enterprise for him, in return for the dissolution of his marriage and for the cardinalship of Rohan, I reply with what I shall say later on about the faith of princes and how it is to be observed. Thus King Louis lost Lombardy through not observing any of those conditions which have been observed by others who have taken provinces and wished to retain them. Nor is this any miracle, but very reasonable and natural. I spoke of this matter with Cardinal Rohan at Nantes when Valentine, as Cesare Borgia, son of Pope Alexander, was commonly called, was occupying the Romagna, for on Cardinal Rohan saying to me that the Italians did not understand war, I replied that the French did not understand politics, for if they did they would never allow the Church to become so great. And experience shows us that the greatness in Italy of the Church and also of Spain have been caused by France, and her ruin has proceeded from them. From which may be drawn a general rule, which never or very rarely fails, that whoever is the cause of another becoming powerful, is ruined himself; for that power is produced by him either through craft or force; and both of these are suspected by the one who has been raised to power.

4

*Why the Kingdom of Darius, Occupied by
Alexander, Did Not Rebel Against
the Successors of the Latter
After His Death*

CONSIDERING THE DIFFICULTIES there are in holding a
newly acquired state, some may wonder how it came to
pass that Alexander the Great became master of Asia in
a few years, and had hardly occupied it when he died,
from which it might be supposed that the whole state
would have rebelled. However, his successors maintained
themselves in possession, and had no further difficulties
in doing so than those which arose among themselves
from their own ambitions.

I reply that the kingdoms known to history have been
governed in two ways: either by a prince and his servants, who, as ministers by his grace and permission, assist
in governing the realm; or by a prince and by barons,
who hold their positions not by favour of the ruler but by
antiquity of blood. Such barons have states and subjects
of their own, who recognise them as their lords, and are
naturally attached to them. In those states which are
governed by a prince and his servants, the prince possesses
more authority, because there is no one in the state regarded as a superior other than himself, and if others are
obeyed it is merely as ministers and officials of the prince,
and no one regards them with any special affection.

Examples of these two kinds of government in our own
time are those of the Turk and the King of France. All
the Turkish monarchy is governed by one ruler, the
others are his servants, and dividing his kingdom into
"sangiacates," he sends to them various administrators,
and changes or recalls them at his pleasure. But the King

of France is surrounded by a large number of ancient nobles, recognised as such by their subjects, and loved by them; they have their prerogatives, of which the king cannot deprive them without danger to himself. Whoever now considers these two states will see that it would be difficult to acquire the state of the Turk; but having conquered it, it would be very easy to hold it. In many respects, on the other hand, it would be easier to conquer the kingdom of France, but there would be great difficulty in holding it.

The causes of the difficulty of occupying the Turkish kingdom are, that the invader could not be invited by princes of that kingdom, nor hope to facilitate his enterprise by the rebellion of those near the ruler's person, as will be evident from reasons given above. Because, being all slaves, and dependent, it will be more difficult to corrupt them, and even if they were corrupted, little effect could be hoped for, as they would not be able to carry the people with them for the reasons mentioned. Therefore, whoever assaults the Turk must be prepared to meet his united forces, and must rely more on his own strength than on the disorders of others; but having once conquered him, and beaten him in battle so that he can no longer raise armies, nothing else is to be feared except the family of the prince, and if this be extinguished, there is no longer any one to be feared, others having no credit with the people; and as the victor before the victory could place no hope in them, so he need not fear them afterwards.

The contrary is the case in kingdoms governed like that of France, because it is easy to enter them by winning over some baron of the kingdom, there being always malcontents, and those desiring innovations. These can, for the reasons stated, open the way to you and facilitate victory; but afterwards, if you wish to keep possession, infinite difficulties arise, both from those who have aided you and from those you have oppressed. Nor is it sufficient to suppress the family of the prince, for there remain those nobles who will take the lead in new revolutions, and being neither able to content them nor ex-

terminate them, you will lose the state whenever an
occasion arises.

Now if you will consider what was the nature of the
government of Darius you will find it similar to the kingdom of the Turk, and therefore Alexander had first to
overthrow it completely and invade the territory, after
which victory, Darius being dead, the state remained secure to Alexander, for the reasons discussed above. And
his successors, had they remained united, might have enjoyed it in peace, nor did any tumults arise in the kingdom except those fomented by themselves. But it is
impossible to possess with such ease countries constituted
like France. Hence arose the frequent rebellions of Spain,
France, and Greece against the Romans, owing to the
numerous principalities which existed in those states; for,
as long as the memory of these lasted, the Romans were
always uncertain of their conquest; but when the memory of these principalities had been extinguished and
with the power and duration of the empire, they became
unchallenged masters. When the Romans fell out
amongst themselves, any one of them could count on the
support of that part of the province where he had established authority. The Romans alone were recognised
as rulers there after the extinction of the old line of
princes. Considering these things, therefore, let no one
be surprised at the facility with which Alexander was able
to hold Asia, and at the difficulties that others have had
in holding conquered territories, like Pyrrhus and many
others; as this was not caused by the greater or lesser
ability of the conqueror, but depended on the dissimilarity of the conditions.

5

The Way to Govern Cities or Dominions That, Previous to Being Occupied, Lived Under Their Own Laws

WHEN THOSE STATES which have been acquired are accustomed to live at liberty under their own laws, there are three ways of holding them. The first is to despoil them; the second is to go and live there in person; the third is to allow them to live under their own laws, taking tribute of them, and creating within the country a government composed of a few who will keep it friendly to you. Because this government, being created by the prince, knows that it cannot exist without his friendship and protection, and will do all it can to keep them. What is more, a city used to liberty can be more easily held by means of its citizens than in any other way, if you wish to preserve it.

There is the example of the Spartans and the Romans. The Spartans held Athens and Thebes by creating within them a government of a few; nevertheless they lost them. The Romans, in order to hold Capua, Carthage, and Numantia, ravaged them, but did not lose them. They wanted to hold Greece in almost the same way as the Spartans held it, leaving it free and under its own laws, but they did not succeed; so that they were compelled to lay waste many cities in that province in order to keep it, because in truth there is no sure method of holding them except by despoiling them. And whoever becomes the ruler of a free city and does not destroy it, can expect to be destroyed by it, for it can always find a motive for rebellion in the name of liberty and of its ancient usages,

46

which are forgotten neither by lapse of time nor by benefits received; and whatever one does or provides, so long as the inhabitants are not separated or dispersed, they do not forget that name and those usages, but appeal to them at once in every emergency, as did Pisa after so many years held in servitude by the Florentines. But when cities or provinces have been accustomed to live under a prince, and the family of that prince is extinguished, being on the one hand used to obey, and on the other not having their old prince, they cannot unite in choosing one from among themselves, and they do not know how to live in freedom, so that they are slower to take arms, and a prince can win them over with greater facility and establish himself securely. But in republics there is greater life, greater hatred, and more desire for vengeance; they do not and cannot cast aside the memory of their ancient liberty, so that the surest way is either to lay them waste or reside in them.

6

Of New Dominions Which Have Been Acquired by One's Own Arms and Ability

LET NO ONE MARVEL if in speaking of new dominions both as to prince and state, I bring forward very exalted instances, for men walk almost always in the paths trodden by others, proceeding in their actions by imitation. Not being always able to follow others exactly, nor attain to the excellence of those he imitates, a prudent man should always follow in the path trodden by great men and imitate those who are most excellent, so that if he does not attain to their greatness, at any rate he will get some tinge of it. He will do as prudent archers, who when the place they wish to hit is too far off, knowing how far their bow will carry, aim at a spot much higher than the one they wish to hit, not in order to reach this height with their arrow, but by help of this high aim to hit the spot they wish to.

I say then that in new dominions, where there is a new prince, it is more or less easy to hold them, according to the greater or lesser ability of him who acquires them. And as the fact of a private individual becoming a prince presupposes either great ability or good fortune, it would apear that either of these things would in part mitigate many difficulties. Nevertheless those who have been less beholden to good fortune have maintained themselves best. The matter is also facilitated by the prince being obliged to reside personally in his territory, having no others. But to come to those who have become princes through their own merits and not by fortune, I regard as the greatest, Moses, Cyrus, Romulus, Theseus, and their like. And although one should not speak of Moses, he having merely carried out what was ordered him by God, still he deserves admiration, if only for that grace which made him worthy to speak with God. But regarding Cyrus and others who have acquired or founded kingdoms, they will all be found worthy of admiration; and if their particular actions and methods are examined they will not appear very different from those of Moses, although he had so great a Master. And in examining their life and deeds it will be seen that they owed nothing to fortune but the opportunity which gave them matter to be shaped into what form they thought fit; and without that opportunity their powers would have been wasted, and without their powers the opportunity would have come in vain.

It was thus necessary that Moses should find the people of Israel slaves in Egypt and oppressed by the Egyptians, so that they were disposed to follow him in order to escape from their servitude. It was necessary that Romulus should be unable to remain in Alba, and should have been exposed at his birth, in order that he might become King of Rome and founder of that nation. It was necessary that Cyrus should find the Persians discontented with the empire of the Medes, and the Medes weak and effeminate through long peace. Theseus could not have shown his abilities if he had not found the Athenians dispersed. These opportunities, therefore, gave these men their chance, and their own great qualities enabled them to profit by them, so as to ennoble their country and augment its fortunes.

Those who by the exercise of abilities such as these become princes, obtain their dominions with difficulty but retain them easily, and the difficulties which they have in acquiring their dominions arise in part from the new rules and regulations that they have to introduce in order to establish their position securely. It must be considered that there is nothing more difficult to carry out, nor more doubtful of success, nor more dangerous to handle, than to initiate a new order of things. For the reformer has enemies in all those who profit by the old order, and only lukewarm defenders in all those who would profit by the new order, this lukewarmness arising partly from fear of their adversaries, who have the laws in their favour; and partly from the incredulity of mankind, who do not truly believe in anything new until they have had actual experience of it. Thus it arises that on every opportunity for attacking the reformer, his opponents do so with the zeal of partisans, the others only defend him half-heartedly, so that between them he runs great danger. It is necessary, however, in order to investigate thoroughly this question, to examine whether these innovators are independent, or whether they depend upon others, that is to say, whether in order to carry out their designs they have to entreat or are able to compel. In the first case they invariably succeed ill, and accomplish nothing; but when they can depend on their own strength and are able to use force, they rarely fail. Thus it comes about that all armed prophets have conquered and unarmed ones failed; for besides what has been already said, the character of peoples varies, and it is easy to persuade them of a thing, but difficult to keep them in that persuasion. And so it is necessary to order things so that when they no longer believe, they can be made to believe by force. Moses, Cyrus, Theseus, and Romulus would not have been able to keep their constitutions observed for so long had they been disarmed, as happened in our own time with Fra Girolamo Savonarola, who failed entirely in his new rules when the multitude began to disbelieve in him, and he had no means of holding fast those who had believed nor of compelling the unbelievers to believe. Therefore such men as these have great difficulty in making their way, and all their dangers are met on the road and must be overcome by their own abilities; but when once they have overcome them and have begun to be held in veneration, and have suppressed those who envied them, they remain powerful and secure, honoured and happy.

To the high examples given I will add a lesser one, which, however, is in some measure comparable and will serve as an instance of all such cases, that of Hiero of

Syracuse, who from a private individual became Prince of Syracuse, without other aid from fortune beyond the opportunity; for the Syracusans being oppressed, elected him as their captain, from which post he rose by ability to be prince; while still in private life his virtues were such that it was written of him, that he lacked nothing to reign but the kingdom. He abolished the old militia, raised a new one, abandoned his old friendships and formed others; and as he had thus friends and soldiers of his own choosing, he was able on this foundation to build securely, so that while he had great trouble in acquiring his position he had little in maintaining it.

7

Of New Dominions Acquired by the Power of Others or by Fortune

THOSE WHO RISE from private citizens to be princes merely by fortune have little trouble in rising but very much in maintaining their position. They meet with no difficulties on the way as they fly over them, but all their difficulties arise when they are established. Such are they who are granted a state either for money, or by favour of him who grants it, as happened to many in Greece, in the cities of Ionia and of the Hellespont, who were created princes by Darius in order to hold these places for his security and glory; such were also those emperors who from private citizens rose to power by bribing the army. Such as these depend absolutely on the good will and fortune of those who have raised them, both of which are extremely inconstant and unstable. They neither know how to, nor are in a position to maintain their rank, for unless he be a man of great genius it is not likely that one who has always lived in a private position should know how to command, and they are unable to maintain themselves because they possess no forces friendly and faithful to them. Moreover, states quickly founded, like all other things of rapid beginnings and growth, cannot have deep roots and wide ramifications, so that the first storm destroys them, unless, as already said, the man who thus becomes a prince is of such great genius as to be able to take immediate steps for maintaining what fortune has thrown into his lap, and lay afterwards those foundations which others make before becoming princes.

With regard to these two methods of becoming a prince,—by ability or by good fortune, I will here adduce two examples which have occurred within our memory, those of Francesco Sforza and Cesare Borgia. Francesco, by appropriate means and through great abilities, from citizen became Duke of Milan, and what he had attained after a thousand difficulties he maintained with little trouble. On the other hand, Cesare Borgia, commonly called Duke Valentine, acquired the state by the influence of his father and lost it when that influence failed, and that although every measure was adopted by him and everything done that a prudent and capable man could do to establish himself firmly in a state that the arms and the favours of others had given him. For, as we have said, he who does not lay his foundations beforehand may by great abilities do so afterwards, although with great trouble to the architect and danger to the building. If, then, one considers the procedure of the duke, it will be seen how firm were the foundations he had laid to his future power, which I do not think is superfluous to examine, as I know of no better precepts for a new prince to follow than may be found in his actions; and if his measures were not successful, it was through no fault of his own but only by the most extraordinary malignity of fortune.

In wishing to aggrandise the duke his son, Alexander VI had to meet very great difficulties both present and future. In the first place, he saw no way of making him ruler of any state that was not a possession of the Church. He knew that the Duke of Milan and the Venetians would not consent in his attempt to take papal cities, because Faenza and Rimini were already under the protection of the Venetians. He saw, moreover, that the military forces of Italy, especially those which might have served him, were in the hands of those who would fear the greatness of the pope, and therefore he could not depend upon them, being all under the command of the Orsini and Colonna and their adherents. It was, therefore, necessary to disturb the existing condition and bring about disorders in the states of Italy in order to obtain secure mastery over a part of them; this was easy, for he found the Venetians, who, actuated by other motives, had invited the French into Italy, which he not

only did not oppose, but facilitated by dissolving the first
marriage of King Louis. The king came thus into Italy
with the aid of the Venetians and the consent of Alexander, and had hardly arrived at Milan before the pope
obtained troops from him for his enterprise in the
Romagna, which was made possible for him thanks to the
reputation of the king. The duke having thus obtained
the Romagna and defeated the Colonna, was hindered by
two things in maintaining it and proceeding further:
the one, his forces, of which he doubted the fidelity; the
other, the will of France; that is to say, he feared lest the
arms of the Orsini of which he had availed himself should
fail him, and not only hinder him in obtaining more but
take from him what he had already conquered, and he
also feared that the king might do the same. He had evi-
dence of this as regards the Orsini when, after taking
Faenza, he assaulted Bologna and observed their back-
wardness in the assault. And as regards the king, he
perceived his designs when, after taking the dukedom
of Urbino, he attacked Tuscany, and the king made him
desist from that enterprise. Whereupon the duke decided
to depend no longer on the fortunes and arms of others.
The first thing he did was to weaken the parties of the
Orsini and Colonna in Rome by gaining all their adherents who were gentlemen and making them his own
followers, by granting them large remuneration, and ap-
pointing them to commands and offices according to
their rank, so that their attachment to their parties was
extinguished in a few months, and entirely concentrated
on the duke. After this he awaited an opportunity for
crushing the chiefs of the Orsini, having already suppressed those of the Colonna family, and when the opportunity arrived he made good use of it, for the Orsini
seeing at length that the greatness of the duke and of the
Church meant their own ruin, convoked a diet at Mag-
ione in the Perugino. Hence sprang the rebellion of Urbino and the tumults in Romagna and infinite dangers
to the duke, who overcame them all with the help of the
French; and having regained his reputation, neither
trusting France nor other foreign forces, in order not to

venture on their alliance, he had recourse to stratagem. He dissembled his aims so well that the Orsini made their peace with him, being represented by Signor Paulo whose suspicions the duke disarmed with every courtesy, presenting him with robes, money, and horses, so that in their simplicity they were induced to come to Sinigaglia and fell into his hands. Having thus suppressed these leaders and made their partisans his friends, the duke had laid a very good foundation to his power, having all the Romagna with the duchy of Urbino, and having gained the favour of the inhabitants, who began to feel the benefit of his rule.

And as this part is worthy of note and of imitation by others, I wil not omit mention of it. When he took the Romagna, it had previously been governed by weak rulers, who had rather despoiled their subjects than governed them, and given them more cause for disunion than for union, so that the province was a prey to robbery, assaults, and every kind of disorder. He, therefore, judged it necessary to give them a good government in order to make them peaceful and obedient to his rule. For this purpose he appointed Messer Remirro de Orco, a cruel and able man, to whom he gave the fullest authority. This man, in a short time, was highly successful in rendering the country orderly and united, whereupon the duke, not deeming such excessive authority expedient, lest it should become hateful, appointed a civil court of justice in the centre of the province under an excellent president, to which each city appointed its own advocate. And as he knew that the harshness of the past had engendered some amount of hatred, in order to purge the minds of the people and to win them over completely, he resolved to show that if any cruelty had taken place it was not by his orders, but through the harsh disposition of his minister. And having found the opportunity he had him cut in half and placed one morning in the public square at Cesena with a piece of wood and blood-stained knife by his side. The ferocity of this spectacle caused the people both satisfaction and amazement. But to return to where we left off.

The duke being now powerful and partly secured against present perils, being armed himself, and having in a great measure put down those neighbouring forces which might injure him, had now to get the respect of France, if he wished to proceed with his acquisitions, for he knew that the king, who had lately discovered his error, would not give him any help. He began therefore to seek fresh alliances and to vacillate with France on the occasion of the expedition that the French were undertaking towards the kingdom of Naples against the Spaniards, who were besieging Gaeta. His intention was to assure himself of them, which he would soon have succeeded in doing if Alexander had lived.

These were the measures taken by him with regard to the present. As to the future, he feared that a new successor to the states of the Church might not be friendly to him and might seek to deprive him of what Alexander had given him, and he sought to provide against this in four ways. First, by destroying all who were of the blood of those ruling families which he had despoiled, in order to deprive the pope of any opportunity. Secondly, by gaining the friendship of the Roman nobles, so that he might through them hold as it were the pope in check. Thirdly, by obtaining as great a hold on the College as he could. Fourthly, by acquiring such power before the pope died as to be able to resist alone the first onslaught. Of these four things he had at the death of Alexander accomplished three, and the fourth he had almost accomplished. For of the dispossessed rulers he killed as many as he could lay hands on, and very few escaped; he had gained to his party the Roman nobles; and he had a great influence in the College. As to new possessions, he designed to become lord of Tuscany, and already possessed Perugia and Piombino, and had assumed the protectorate over Pisa; and as he had no longer to fear the French (for the French had been deprived of the kingdom of Naples by the Spaniards in such a way that both parties were obliged to buy his friendship) he seized Pisa. After this, Lucca and Siena at once yielded, partly through hate of the Florentines and partly through fear; the Florentines had no resources, so that, had he succeeded as he had done before, in the very year that Alexander died he would have gained such strength and renown as to be able to maintain himself without depending on the fortunes or strength of others, but solely by his own power and ability. But Alexander died five years after Cesare Borgia had first drawn his sword. He was left with only the state of Romagna firmly established, and all the other schemes in midair, between two very powerful and hostile armies, and suffering from a fatal illness. But the valour and ability of the duke were such, and he knew so well how to win over men or vanquish them, and so strong were the foundations that he had laid in this short time, that if he had not had those two armies upon him, or else had been in good health, he would have survived every difficulty. And that his foundations were good is seen from the fact that the Romagna waited for him more than a month in Rome, although half dead, he remained secure, and although the Baglioni, Vitelli, and Orsini entered Rome they found no followers against him. He was able, if not to make pope whom he wished, at any rate to prevent a pope being created whom he did not wish. But if at the death of Alexander he had been well, everything would have been easy. And he told me on the day that Pope Julius II was elected, that he had thought of everything which might happen on the death of his father, and provided against everything, except that he had never thought that at his father's death he would be dying himself.

Reviewing thus all the actions of the duke, I find nothing to blame, on the contrary, I feel bound, as I have done, to hold him up as an example to be imitated by all who by fortune and with the arms of others have risen to power. For with his great courage and high ambition he could not have acted otherwise, and his designs were only frustrated by the short life of Alexander and his own illness. Whoever, therefore, deems it necessary in his new principality to secure himself against enemies, to gain friends, to conquer by force or fraud, to make himself beloved and feared by the people, followed and reverenced by the soldiers, to destroy those who can and may injure him, introduce innovations into old customs, to be severe and kind, magnanimous and liberal, suppress the old militia, create a new one, maintain the friendship of kings and princes in such a way that they are glad to benefit him and fear to injure him, such a one can find no better example than the actions of this man. The only thing he can be accused of is that in the creation of Julius II he made a bad choice; for, as has been said, not being able to choose his own pope, he could still prevent any one individual being made pope, and he ought never to have permitted any of those cardinals to be raised to the papacy whom he had injured, or who when pope would stand in fear of him. For men commit injuries either through fear or through hate. Those whom he had injured were, among others, San Pietro ad Vincula, Colonna, San Giorgio, and Ascanio. All the others, if elected to the pontificate, would have had to fear him except Rohan and the Spaniards; the latter through their relationship and obligations to him, the former from his great power, being related to the King of France. For these reasons the duke ought above all things to have created a Spaniard pope; and if unable, then he should have consented to Rohan being appointed and not San Pietro ad Vincula. And whoever thinks that in high personages new benefits cause old offences to be forgotten, makes a great mistake. The duke, therefore, erred in this choice, and it was the cause of his ultimate ruin.

8

Of Those Who Have Attained the Position of Prince by Villainy

But as there are still two ways of becoming prince which cannot be attributed entirely either to fortune or to ability, they must not be passed over, although one of them could be more fully discussed if we were treating of republics. These are when one becomes prince by some nefarious or villainous means, or when a private citizen becomes the prince of his country through the favour of his fellow-citizens. And in speaking of the former means, I will give two examples, one ancient, the other modern, without entering further into the merits of this method, as I judge them to be sufficient for any one obliged to imitate them.

Agathocles the Sicilian rose not only from private life but from the lowest and most abject position to be King of Syracuse. The son of a potter, he led a life of the utmost wickedness through all the stages of his fortune. Nevertheless, his wickedness was accompanied by such vigour of mind and body that, having joined the militia, he rose through its ranks to be prætor of Syracuse. Having been appointed to this position, and having decided to become prince, and to hold with violence and without the support of others that which had been constitutionally granted him; and having imparted his design to Hamilcar the Carthaginian, who was fighting with his armies in Sicily, he called together one morning the people and senate of Syracuse, as if he had to deliberate on matters of importance to the republic, and at a given signal had all the senators and the richest men of the people killed by his soldiers. After their death he occupied and held rule over the city without any civil strife. And although he was twice beaten by the Carthaginians and ultimately besieged, he was able not only to defend the city, but leaving a portion of his forces for its defence, with the remainder he invaded Africa, and in a short time liberated Syracuse from the siege and brought the Carthaginians to great extremities, so that they were obliged to come to terms with him, and remain contented with the possession of Africa, leaving Sicily to Agathocles. Whoever considers, therefore, the actions and qualities of this man, will see few if any things which can be attributed to fortune; for, as above stated, it was not by the favour of any person, but through the grades of the militia, in which he had advanced with a thousand hardships and perils, that he arrived at the position of prince, which he afterwards maintained by so many courageous and perilous expedients. It cannot be called virtue to kill one's fellow-citizens, betray one's friends, be without faith, without pity, and without religion; by these methods one may indeed gain power, but not glory. For if the virtues of Agathocles in braving and overcoming perils, and his greatness of soul in supporting and surmounting obstacles be considered, one sees no reason for holding him inferior to any of the most renowned captains. Nevertheless his barbarous cruelty and inhumanity, together with his countless atrocities, do not permit of his being named among the most famous men. We cannot attribute to fortune or virtue that which he achieved without either.

In our own times, during the pontificate of Alexander VI, Oliverotto da Fermo had been left as a young fatherless boy under the care of his maternal uncle, Giovanni Fogliani, who brought him up, and sent him in early youth to soldier under Paolo Vitelli, in order that he might, trained in that hard school, obtain a good military position. On the death of Paolo he fought under his brother Vitellozzo, and in a very short time, being of great intelligence, and active in mind and body, he became one of the leaders of his troops. But deeming it servile to be under others, he resolved, with the help of some citizens of Fermo, who preferred servitude to the liberty of their country, and with the favour of the Vitelli, to occupy Fermo; he therefore wrote to Giovanni Fogliani, how, having been for many years away from home, he wished to come to see him and his city, and as far as possible to inspect his estates. And as he had only laboured to gain honour, in order that his fellow-citizens might see that he had not spent his time in vain, he wished to come honourably accompanied by one hundred horsemen, his friends and followers, and prayed him that he would be pleased to order that he should be received with honour by the citizens of Fermo, by which he would honour not only him, Oliverotto, but also himself, as he had been his pupil. Giovanni did not fail in any due courtesy towards his nephew; he caused him to be honourably received by the people of Fermo, and lodged him in his own house. After waiting some days to arrange all that was necessary to his villainous projects, Oliverotto invited Giovanni Fogliani and all the principal men of Fermo to a grand banquet. After the dinner and the entertainments usual at such feasts, Oliverotto artfully introduced certain important matters of discussion, speaking of the greatness of Pope Alexander, and of his son Cesare, and of their enterprises. To which discourses Giovanni and others having replied, he all at once rose, saying that these matters should be spoken of in a more private place, and withdrew into a room where Giovanni and the other citizens followed him. They were no sooner seated than soldiers rushed out of hiding-places and killed Giovanni and all the others. After which massacre Oliverotto mounted his horse, rode through the town and besieged the chief magistrate in his place, so that through fear they were obliged to obey him and form a government, of which he made himself prince. And all those being dead who, if discontented, could injure him, he fortified himself with new orders, civil and military, in such a way that within the year that he held the principality he was not only safe himself in the city of Fermo, but had become formidable to all his neighbours. And his overthrow would have been difficult, like that of Agathocles, if he had not allowed himself to be deceived by Cesare Borgia, when he captured the Orsini and Vitelli at Sinigaglia, as already related, where he also was taken, one year after the parricide he had committed, and strangled, together with Vitellozzo, who had been his teacher in ability and atrocity.

Some may wonder how it came about that Agathocles, and others like him, could, after infinite treachery and cruelty, live secure for many years in their country and defend themselves from external enemies without being conspired against by their subjects; although many others have, owing to their cruelty, been unable to maintain their position in times of peace, not to speak of the uncertain times of war. I believe this arises from the cruelties being exploited well or badly. Well committed may be called those (if it is permissible to use the word well of evil) which are perpetrated once for the need of securing one's self, and which afterwards are not persisted in, but are exchanged for measures as useful to the subjects as possible. Cruelties ill committed are those which, although at first few, increase rather than diminish with time. Those who follow the former method may remedy in some measure their condition, both with God and man; as did Agathocles. As to the others, it is impossible for them to maintain themselves.

Whence it is to be noted, that in taking a state the conqueror must arrange to commit all his cruelties at once, so as not to have to recur to them every day, and so as to be able, by not making fresh changes, to reassure people and win them over by benefiting them. Whoever acts otherwise, either through timidity or bad counsel, is always obliged to stand with knife in hand, and can never depend on his subjects, because they, owing to continually fresh injuries, are unable to depend upon him. For injuries should be done all together, so that being less tasted, they will give less offence. Benefits should be granted little by little, so that they may be better enjoyed. And above all, a prince must live with his subjects in such a way that no accident of good or evil fortune can deflect him from his course; for necessity arising in adverse times, you are not in time with severity, and the good that you do does not profit, as it is judged to be forced upon you, and you will derive no benefit whatever from it.

9

Of the Civic Principality

BUT WE NOW COME to the case where a citizen becomes
prince not through crime or intolerable violence, but
by the favour of his fellow-citizens, which may be called
a civic principality. To attain this position depends not
entirely on worth or entirely on fortune, but rather on
cunning assisted by fortune. One attains it by help of
popular favour or by the favour of the aristocracy. For
in every city these two opposite parties are to be found,
arising from the desire of the populace to avoid the
oppression of the great, and the desire of the great to
command and oppress the people. And from these two
opposing interests arises in the city one of the three
effects: either absolute government, liberty, or licence.
The former is created either by the populace or the
nobility, depending on the relative opportunities of the
two parties; for when the nobility see that they are unable
to resist the people they unite in exalting one of their
number and creating him prince, so as to be able to carry
out their own designs under the shadow of his authority.
The populace, on the other hand, when unable to resist
the nobility, endeavour to exalt and create a prince in
order to be protected by his authority. He who becomes
prince by help of the nobility has greater difficulty in
maintaining his power than he who is raised by the
populace, for he is surrounded by those who think themselves his equals, and is thus unable to direct or command
as he pleases. But one who is raised to leadership by
popular favour finds himself alone, and has no one, or
very few, who are not ready to obey him. Besides which,
it is impossible to satisfy the nobility by fair dealing and
without inflicting injury on others, whereas it is very
easy to satisfy the mass of the people in this way. For

the aim of the people is more honest than that of the nobility, the latter desiring to oppress, and the former merely to avoid oppression. It must also be added that the prince can never insure himself against a hostile populace on account of their number, but he can against the hostility of the great, as they are but few. The worst that a prince has to expect from a hostile people is to be abandoned, but from hostile nobles he has to fear not only desertion but their active opposition, and as they are more far-seeing and more cunning, they are always in time to save themselves and take sides with the one who they expect will conquer. The prince is, moreover, obliged to live always with the same people, but he can easily do without the same nobility, being able to make and unmake them at any time, and improve their position or deprive them of it as he pleases.

And to throw further light on this part of my argument, I would say, that the nobles are to be considered in two different manners; that is, they are either to be ruled so as to make them entirely dependent on your fortunes, or else not. Those that are thus bound to you and are not rapacious, must be honoured and loved; those who stand aloof must be considered in two ways, they either do this through pusillanimity and natural want of courage, and in this case you ought to make use of them, and especially such as are of good counsel, so that they may honour you in prosperity and in adversity you have not to fear them. But when they are not bound to you of set purpose and for ambitious ends, it is a sign that they think more of themselves than of you; and from such men the prince must guard himself and look upon them as secret enemies, who will help to ruin him when in adversity.

One, however, who becomes prince by favour of the populace, must maintain its friendship, which he will find easy, the people asking nothing but not to be oppressed. But one who against the people's wishes becomes prince by favour of the nobles, should above all endeavour to gain the favour of the people; this will be easy to him if he protects them. And as men, who receive good from whom they expected evil, feel under a greater obligation to their benefactor, so the populace will soon become even better disposed towards him than if he had become prince through their favour. The prince can win their favour in many ways, which vary according to circumstances, for which no certain rule can be given, and will therefore be passed over. I will only say, in conclusion, that it is necessary for a prince to possess the friendship of the people; otherwise he has no resource in times of adversity.

Nabis, prince of the Spartans, sustained a siege by the whole of Greece and a victorious Roman army, and defended his country against them and maintained his own position. It sufficed when the danger arose for him to make sure of a few, which would not have sufficed if the populace had been hostile to him. And let no one oppose my opinion in this by quoting the trite proverb, "He who builds on the people, builds on mud"; because that is true when a private citizen relies upon the people and persuades himself that they will liberate him if he is oppressed by enemies or by the magistrates; in this case he might often find himself deceived, as were in Rome the Gracchi and in Florence Messer Georgio Scali. But when it is a prince who founds himself on this basis, one who can command and is a man of courage, and does not get frightened in adversity, and does not neglect other preparations, and one who by his own valour and measures animates the mass of the people, he will not find himself deceived by them, and he will find that he has laid his foundations well.

Usually these principalities are in danger when the prince from the position of a civil ruler changes to an absolute one, for these princes either command themselves or by means of magistrates. In the latter case their position is weaker and more dangerous, for they are at the mercy of those citizens who are appointed magistrates, who can, especially in times of adversity, with great facility deprive them of their position, either by acting against them or by not obeying them. The prince is not in time, in such dangers, to assume absolute authority, for the citizens and subjects who are accustomed to take their orders from the magistrates are not ready in these emergencies to obey his, and he will always in difficult times lack men whom he can rely on. Such a prince cannot base himself on what he sees in quiet times, when the citizens have need of the state; for then every one is full of promises and each one is ready to die for him when death is far off; but in adversity, when the state has need of citizens, then he will find but few. And this experience is the more dangerous, in that it can only be had once. Therefore a wise prince will seek means by which his subjects will always and in every possible condition of things have need of his government, and then they will always be faithful to him.

10

How the Strength of All States
Should Be Measured

IN EXAMINING the character of these principalities it is necessary to consider another point, namely, whether the prince has such position as to be able in case of need to maintain himself alone, or whether he has always need of the protection of others. The better to explain this I would say, that I consider those capable of maintaining themselves alone who can, through abundance of men or money, put together a sufficient army, and hold the field against any one who assails them; and I consider to have need of others, those who cannot take the field against their enemies, but are obliged to take refuge within their walls and stand on the defensive. We have already discussed the former case and will speak of it in future as occasion arises. In the second case there is nothing to be said except to encourage such a prince to provision and fortify his own town, and not to trouble about the surrounding country. And whoever has strongly fortified his town and, as regards the government of his subjects, has proceeded as we have already described and will further relate, will be attacked with great reluctance, for men are always averse to enterprises in which they foresee difficulties, and it can never appear easy to attack one who has his town stoutly defended and is not hated by the people.

The cities of Germany are absolutely free, have little surrounding country, and obey the emperor when they choose, and they do not fear him or any other potentate that they have about them. They are fortified in such a manner that every one thinks that to reduce them would be tedious and difficult, for they all have the necessary moats and bastions, sufficient artillery, and always keep food, drink, and fuel for one year in the public storehouses. Beyond which, to keep the lower classes satisfied, and without loss to the commonwealth, they have always enough means to give them work for one year in these employments which form the nerve and life of the town, and in the industries by which the lower classes live. Military exercises are still held in high reputation, and many regulations are in force for maintaining them.

A prince, therefore, who possesses a strong city and does not make himself hated, cannot be assaulted; and if he were to be so, the assailant would be obliged to retire shamefully; for so many things change, that it is almost impossible for any one to maintain a siege for a year with his armies idle. And to those who urge that the people, having their possessions outside and seeing them burnt, will not have patience, and the long siege and self-interest will make them forget their prince, I reply that a powerful and courageous prince will always overcome those difficulties by now raising the hopes of his subjects that the evils will not last long, now impressing them with fear of the enemy's cruelty, now by dextrously assuring himself of those who appear too bold. Besides which, the enemy would naturally burn and ravage the country on first arriving and at the time when men's minds are still hot and eager to defend themselves, and therefore the prince has still less to fear, for after some time, when people have cooled down, the damage is done, the evil has been suffered, and there is no remedy, so that they are the more ready to unite with their prince, as it appears that he is under an obligation to them, their houses having been burnt and their possessions ruined in his defence.

It is the nature of men to be as much bound by the benefits that they confer as by those they receive. From which it follows that, everything considered, a prudent prince will not find it difficult to uphold the courage of his subjects both at the commencement and during a state of siege, if he possesses provisions and means to defend himself.

11

Of Ecclesiastical Principalities

IT NOW ONLY REMAINS to us to speak of ecclesiastical principalities, with regard to which the difficulties lie wholly before they are possessed. They are acquired either by ability or by fortune; but are maintained without either, for they are sustained by ancient religious customs, which are so powerful and of such quality, that they keep their princes in power in whatever manner they proceed and live. These princes alone have states without defending them, have subjects without governing them, and their states, not being defended, are not taken from them; their subjects not being governed do not resent it, and neither think nor are capable of alienating themselves from them. Only these principalities, therefore, are secure and happy. But as they are upheld by higher causes, which the human mind cannot attain to, I will abstain from speaking of them; for being exalted and maintained by God, it would be the work of a presumptuous and foolish man to discuss them. However, I might be asked how it has come about that the Church has reached such great temporal power, when, previous to Alexander VI, the Italian potentates—and not merely the really powerful ones, but every lord or baron, however insignificant—held it in slight esteem as regards temporal power; whereas now it is dreaded by a king of France, whom it has been able to drive out of Italy, and has also been able to ruin the Venetians. Therefore, although this is well known, I do not think it superfluous to call it to mind.

Before Charles, King of France, came into Italy, this country was under the rule of the Pope, the Venetians, the King of Naples, the Duke of Milan, and the Florentines. These potentates had to have two chief cares:

one, that no foreigner should enter Italy by force of
arms, the other that none of the existing governments
should extend its dominions. Those chiefly to be watched
were the Pope and the Venetians. To keep back the
Venetians required the alliance of all the others, as in
the defence of Ferrara, and to keep down the Pope they
made use of the Roman barons. These were divided into
two factions, the Orsini and the Colonna, and as there
was constant quarrelling between them, and they were
constantly under arms, before the eyes of the Pope, they
kept the papacy weak and infirm. And although there
arose now and then a resolute Pope like Sextus, yet his
fortune or ability was never able to liberate him from
these evils. The shortness of their life was the reason of
this, for in the course of ten years which, as a general
rule, a Pope lived, he had great difficulty in suppressing
even one of the factions, and if, for example, a Pope had
almost put down the Colonna, a new Pope would succeed
who was hostile to the Orsini, which caused the Colonna
to spring up again, and he was not in time to suppress
them.

This caused the temporal power of the Pope to be of
little esteem in Italy. Then arose Alexander VI who, of
all the pontiffs who have ever reigned, best showed how
a Pope might prevail both by money and by force. With
Duke Valentine as his instrument, and seizing the opportunity of the French invasion, he did all that I have
previously described in speaking of the actions of the
duke. And although his object was to aggrandise not
the Church but the duke, what he did resulted in the
aggrandisement of the Church, which after the death
of the duke became the heir of his labours. Then came
Pope Julius, who found the Church powerful, possessing
all Romagna, all the Roman barons suppressed, and the
factions destroyed by the severity of Alexander. He also
found the way open for accumulating wealth in ways
never used before the time of Alexander. These measures
were not only followed by Julius, but increased; he
resolved to gain Bologna, put down the Venetians and
drive the French from Italy, in all which enterprises he

was successful. He merits the greater praise, as he did everything to increase the power of the Church and not of any private person. He also kept the Orsini and Colonna parties in the condition in which he found them, and although there were some leaders among them who might have made changes, there were two things that kept them steady: one, the greatness of the Church, which they dreaded; the other, the fact that they had no cardinals, who are the origin of the tumults among them. For these parties are never at rest when they have cardinals, for these stir up the parties both within Rome and outside, and the barons are forced to defend them. Thus from the ambitions of prelates arise the discords and tumults among the barons. His holiness, Pope Leo X, therefore, has found the pontificate in a very powerful condition, from which it is hoped that as those Popes made it great by force of arms, so he through his goodness and infinite other virtues will make it both great and venerated.

12

The Different Kinds of Militia and Mercenary Soldiers

HAVING NOW DISCUSSED FULLY the qualities of these principalities of which I proposed to treat, and partially considered the causes of their prosperity or failure, and having also showed the methods by which many have sought to obtain such states, it now remains for me to treat generally of the methods, both offensive and defensive, that can be used in each of them. We have said already how necessary it is for a prince to have his foundations good, otherwise he is certain to be ruined. The chief foundations of all states, whether new, old, or mixed, are good laws and good arms. And as there cannot be good laws where there are not good arms, and where there are good arms there must be good laws, I will not now discuss the laws, but will speak of the arms.

I say, therefore, that the arms by which a prince defends his possessions are either his own, or else mercenaries, or auxiliaries, or mixed. The mercenaries and auxiliaries are useless and dangerous, and if any one supports his state by the arms of mercenaries, he will never stand firm or sure, as they are disunited, ambitious, without discipline, faithless, bold amongst friends, cowardly amongst enemies, they have no fear of God, and keep no faith with men. Ruin is only deferred as long as the assault is postponed; in peace you are despoiled by them, and in war by the enemy. The cause of this is that they have no love or other motive to keep them in the field beyond a trifling wage, which is not enough to make them ready to die for you. They are quite willing to be your soldiers so long as you do not make war, but when war comes, it is either fly or decamp altogether. I ought to have little trouble in proving this,

since the ruin of Italy is now caused by nothing else but
through her having relied for many years on mercenary
arms. These did indeed help certain individuals to power,
and appeared courageous when matched against each
other, but when the foreigner came they showed their
worthlessness. Thus it came about that King Charles of
France was allowed to take Italy without the slightest
trouble, and those who said that it was owing to our
sins, spoke the truth, but it was not the sins they meant
but those that I have related. And as it was the sins of
princes, they too have suffered the punishment.

I will explain more fully the defects of these arms.
Mercenary captains are either very capable men or not;
if they are, you cannot rely upon them, for they will always aspire to their own greatness, either by oppressing
you, their master, or by oppressing others against your
intentions; but if the captain is not an able man, he
will generally ruin you. And if it is replied to this, that
whoever has armed forces will do the same, whether
these are mercenary or not, I would reply that as armies
are to be used either by a prince or by a republic, the
prince must go in person to take the position of captain, and the republic must send its own citizens. If the
man sent turns out incompetent, it must change him;
and if capable, keep him by law from going beyond
the proper limits. And it is seen by experience that only
princes and armed republics make very great progress,
whereas mercenary forces do nothing but harm, and
also an armed republic submits less easily to the rule of
one of its citizens than a republic armed by foreign
forces.

Rome and Sparta were for many centuries well armed
and free. The Swiss are well armed and enjoy great
freedom. As an example of mercenary armies in antiquity there are the Carthaginians, who were oppressed
by their mercenary soldiers, after the termination of the
first war with the Romans, even while they still had
their own citizens as captains. Philip of Macedon was
made captain of their forces by the Thebans after the
death of Epaminondas, and after gaining the victory he

deprived them of liberty. The Milanese, on the death
of Duke Philip, hired Francesco Sforza against the Venetians, who having overcome the enemy at Caravaggio,
allied himself with them to oppress the Milanese his
own employers. The father of this Sforza, being a soldier
in the service of Queen Giovanna of Naples, left her
suddenly unarmed, by which she was compelled, in order
not to lose the kingdom, to throw herself into the arms
of the King of Aragon. And if the Venetians and Florentines have in times past increased their dominions by
means of such forces, and their captains have not made
themselves princes but have defended them, I reply that
the Florentines in this case have been favoured by chance,
for of the capable leaders whom they might have feared,
some did not conquer, some met with opposition, and
others directed their ambition elsewhere. The one who
did not conquer was Sir John Hawkwood, whose fidelity
could not be known as he was not victorious, but every
one will admit that, had he conquered, the Florentines
would have been at his mercy. Sforza had always the
Bracceschi against him which served as a mutual check.
Francesco directed his ambition towards Lombardy; Braccio against the Church and the kingdom of Naples.

But let us look at what occurred a short time ago.
The Florentines appointed Paolo Vitelli their captain,
a man of great prudence, who had risen from a private
station to the highest reputation. If he had taken Pisa no
one can deny that it was highly important for the Florentines to retain his friendship, because had he become
the soldier of their enemies they would have had no
means of opposing him; and if they had retained him
they would have been obliged to obey him. As to the
Venetians, if one considers the progress they made, it will
be seen that they acted surely and gloriously so long
as they made war with their own forces; that it was
before they commenced their enterprises on land that
they fought courageously with their own gentlemen and
armed populace, but when they began to fight on land
they abandoned this virtue, and began to follow the
Italian custom. And at the commencement of their land

conquests they had not much to fear from their captains, their territories not being very large, and their reputation being great, but as their possessions increased, as they did under Carmagnola, they had an example of their mistake. For seeing that he was very powerful, after he had defeated the Duke of Milan, and knowing, on the other hand, that he was but lukewarm in this war, they considered that they would not make any more conquests with him, and they neither would nor could dismiss him, for fear of losing what they had already gained. In order to make sure of him they were therefore obliged to execute him. They then had for captains Bartolommeo da Bergamo, Roberto da San Severino, Count di Pitigliano, and such like, from whom they had to fear loss instead of gain, as happened subsequently at Vailà, where in one day they lost what they had laboriously gained in eight hundred years; for with these forces, only slow and trifling acquisitions are made, but sudden and miraculous losses. And as I have cited these examples from Italy, which has now for many years been governed by mercenary forces, I will now deal more largely with them, so that having seen their origin and progress, they can be better remedied.

You must understand that in these latter times, as soon as the empire began to be repudiated in Italy and the Pope to gain greater reputation in temporal matters, Italy was divided into many states; many of the principal cities took up arms against their nobles, who, favoured by the emperor, had held them in subjection, and the Church encouraged this in order to increase its temporal power. In many other cities one of the inhabitants became prince. Thus Italy having fallen almost entirely into the hands of the Church and a few republics, and the priests and other citizens not being accustomed to bear arms, they began to hire foreigners as soldiers. The first to bring into reputation this kind of militia was Alberigo da Como, a native of Romagna. Braccio and Sforza, who were in their day the arbiters of Italy were, amongst others, trained by him. After these came all those others who up to the present day have commanded the armies of Italy, and the result of their prowess has been that Italy has been overrun by Charles, preyed on by Louis, tyrannised over by Ferrando, and insulted by the Swiss. The system adopted by them was, in the first place, to increase their own reputation by discrediting the infantry. They did this because, as they had no country and lived on their earnings, a few foot soldiers did not augment their reputation, and they could not maintain a large number and therefore they restricted themselves almost entirely to cavalry, by which with a smaller number they were well paid and honoured. They reduced things to such a state that in an army of 20,000 soldiers there were not 2,000 foot. They had also used every means to spare themselves and the soldiers any hardship or fear by not killing each other in their encounters, but taking prisoners without expectation of ransom. They made no attacks on fortifications by night; and those in the fortifications did not attack the tents at night, they made no stockades or ditches around their camps, and did not take the field in winter. All these things were permitted by their military code, and adopted, as we have said, to avoid trouble and danger, so that they have reduced Italy to slavery and degradation.

13

Of Auxiliary, Mixed, and Native Troops

WHEN ONE ASKS a powerful neighbour to come to aid and
defend one with his forces, they are termed auxiliaries
and are as useless as mercenaries. This was done in recent
times by Julius, who seeing the wretched failure of his
mercenary forces, in his Ferrara enterprise, had recourse
to auxiliaries, and arranged with Ferrando, King of
Spain, that he should help him with his armies. These
forces may be good in themselves, but they are always
dangerous for those who borrow them, for if they lose
you are defeated, and if they conquer you remain their
prisoner. And although ancient history is full of examples
of this, I will not depart from the example of Pope
Julius II, which is still fresh. Nothing could be less prudent than the course he adopted; for, wishing to take
Ferrara, he put himself entirely into the power of a
foreigner. But by good fortune there arose a third cause
which prevented him reaping the effects of his bad policy;
for when his auxiliaries were beaten at Ravenna, the
Swiss rose up and drove back the victors, against all expectation of himself or others, so that he was not taken
prisoner by the enemy which had fled, nor by his own
auxiliaries, having conquered by other arms than theirs.
The Florentines, being totally disarmed, hired 10,000
Frenchmen to attack Pisa, by which measure they ran
greater risk than at any period of their struggles. The
emperor of Constantinople, to oppose his neighbours, put
10,000 Turks into Greece, who after the war would not
go away again, which was the beginning of the servitude
of Greece to the infidels.

And one, therefore, who wishes not to conquer, would
do well to use these forces, which are much more danger-

77

ous than mercenaries, as with them ruin is complete, for they are all united, and owe obedience to others, whereas with mercenaries, when they have conquered, it requires more time and a good opportunity for them to injure you, as they do not form a single body and have been engaged and paid by you, therefore a third party that you have made leader cannot at once acquire enough authority to be able to injure you. In a word, the greatest danger with mercenaries lies in their cowardice and reluctance to fight, but with auxiliaries the danger lies in their courage.

A wise prince, therefore, always avoids these forces and has recourse to his own, and would prefer rather to lose with his own men than conquer with the forces of others, not deeming it a true victory which is gained by foreign arms. I never hesitate to cite the example of Cesare Borgia and his actions. This duke entered Romagna with auxiliary troops, leading forces composed entirely of French soldiers, and with these he took Imola and Forlì; but as they seemed unsafe, he had recourse to mercenaries as a less risky policy, and hired the Orsini and Vitelli. Afterwards finding these uncertain to handle, unfaithful, and dangerous, he suppressed them, and relied upon his own men. And the difference between these forces can be easily seen if one considers the difference between the reputation of the duke when he had only the French, when he had the Orsini and Vitelli, and when he had to rely on himself and his own soldiers. His reputation will be found to have constantly increased, and he was never so highly esteemed as when every one saw that he was the sole master of his forces.

I do not wish to depart from recent Italian instances, but I cannot omit Hiero of Syracuse, whom I have already mentioned. This man being, as I said, made head of the army by the Syracusans, immediately recognised the uselessness of that militia which was organized like our Italian mercenary troops, and as he thought it unsafe either to retain them or dismiss them, he had them cut in pieces and thenceforward made war with his own arms and not those of others. I would also call to mind a symbolic tale from the Old Testament which well illustrates this point. When David offered to Saul to go and fight against the Philistine champion Goliath, Saul, to encourage him, armed him with his own arms, which when David had tried on, he refused saying, that with them he could not fight so well; he preferred, therefore, to face the enemy with his own sling and knife. In short, the arms of others either fail, overburden, or else impede you. Charles VII, father of King Louis XI, having through good fortune and bravery liberated France from the English, recognised this necessity of being armed with his own forces, and established in his kingdom a system of men-at-arms and infantry. Afterwards King Louis his son abolished the infantry and began to hire Swiss, which mistake being followed by others is, as may now be seen, a cause of danger to that kingdom. For by giving such reputation to the Swiss, France has disheartened all her own troops, the infantry having been abolished and the men-at-arms being obliged to foreigners for assistance; for being accustomed to fight with Swiss troops, they think they cannot conquer without them. Whence it comes that the French are insufficiently strong to oppose the Swiss, and without the aid of the Swiss they will not venture against others. The armies of the French are thus of a mixed kind, partly mercenary and partly her own; taken together they are much better than troops entirely composed of mercenaries or auxiliaries, but much inferior to national forces.

And let this example be sufficient, for the kingdom of France would be invincible if Charles's military organization had been developed or maintained. But men with their lack of prudence initiate novelties and, finding the first taste good, do not notice the poison within, as I pointed out previously in regard to wasting fevers.

The prince, therefore, who fails to recognize troubles in his state as they arise, is not truly wise, and it is given to few to be thus. If we consider the first cause of the collapse of the Roman Empire we shall find it merely due to the hiring of Goth mercenaries, for from that time we find the Roman strength begins to weaken. All the advantages derived from the Empire fell to the Goths.

I conclude then by saying that no prince is secure without his own troops, on the contrary he is entirely dependent on fortune, having no trustworthy means of defence in time of trouble. It has always been held and proclaimed by wise men *quod nihil sit tam infirmum aut instabile quam fama potentiae non sua vi nixae.* One's own troops are those composed either of subjects or of citizens or of one's own dependants; all others are mercenaries or auxiliaries. The way to organise one's own troops is easily learnt if the methods of the four princes mentioned above be studied, and if one considers how Philip, father of Alexander the Great, and many republics and sovereigns have organised theirs. With such examples as these there is no need to labour the point.

14

The Duties of a Prince with Regard to the Militia

A PRINCE SHOULD THEREFORE have no other aim or
thought, nor take up any other thing for his study, but
war and its organisation and discipline, for that is the
only art that is necessary to one who commands, and it
is of such virtue that it not only maintains those who are
born princes, but often enables men of private fortune
to attain to that rank. And one sees, on the other hand,
that when princes think more of luxury than of arms,
they lose their state. The chief cause of the loss of states,
is the contempt of this art, and the way to acquire them
is to be well versed in the same.

Francesco Sforza, through being well armed, became,
from private status, Duke of Milan; his sons, through
wishing to avoid the fatigue and hardships of war,
from dukes became private persons. For among other
evils caused by being disarmed, it renders you contemptible; which is one of those disgraceful things which
a prince must guard against, as will be explained later.
Because there is no comparison whatever between an
armed and a disarmed man; it is not reasonable to sup-
pose that one who is armed will obey willingly one who
is unarmed; or that any unarmed man will remain safe
among armed servants. For one being disdainful and
the other suspicious, it is not possible for them to act
well together. And therefore a prince who is ignorant
of military matters, besides the other misfortunes already mentioned, cannot be esteemed by his soldiers,
nor have confidence in them.

He ought, therefore, never to let his thoughts stray
from the exercise of war; and in peace he ought to

practise it more than in war, which he can do in two
ways: by action and by study. As to action, he must,
besides keeping his men well disciplined and exer-
cised, engage continually in hunting, and thus accus-
tom his body to hardships; and meanwhile learn the
nature of the land, how steep the mountains are, how
the valleys debouch, where the plains lie, and understand the nature of rivers and swamps. To all this he
should devote great attention. This knowledge is useful in two ways. In the first place, one learns to know
one's country, and can the better see how to defend it.
Then by means of the knowledge and experience
gained in one locality, one can easily understand any
other that it may be necessary to observe; for the hills
and valleys, plains and rivers of Tuscany, for instance,
have a certain resemblance to those of other provinces,
so that from a knowledge of the country in one province
one can easily arrive at a knowledge of others. And
that prince who is lacking in this skill is wanting in
the first essentials of a leader; for it is this which teaches
how to find the enemy, take up quarters, lead armies,
plan battles and lay siege to towns with advantage.

Philopœmen, prince of the Achaei, among other
praises bestowed on him by writers, is lauded because
in times of peace he thought of nothing but the methods of warfare, and when he was in the country with
his friends, he often stopped and asked them: If the
enemy were on that hill and we found ourselves here
with our army, which of us would have the advantage?
How could we safely approach him maintaining our
order? If we wished to retire, what ought we to do? If
they retired, how should we follow them? And he put
before them as they went along all the contingencies
that might happen to an army, heard their opinion,
gave his own, fortifying it by argument; so that thanks
to these constant reflections there could never happen
any incident when actually leading his armies for which
he was not prepared.

But as to exercise for the mind, the prince ought to
read history and study the actions of eminent men, see

how they acted in warfare, examine the causes of their victories and defeats in order to imitate the former and avoid the latter, and above all, do as some men have done in the past, who have imitated some one, who has been much praised and glorified, and have always kept his deeds and actions before them, as they say Alexander the Great imitated Achilles, Cæsar Alexander, and Scipio Cyrus. And whoever reads the life of Cyrus written by Xenophon, will perceive in the life of Scipio how gloriously he imitated the former, and how, in chastity, affability, humanity, and liberality Scipio conformed to those qualities of Cyrus as described by Xenophon.

A wise prince should follow similar methods and never remain idle in peaceful times, but industriously make good use of them, so that when fortune changes she may find him prepared to resist her blows, and to prevail in adversity.

15

Of the Things for Which Men, and Especially Princes, Are Praised or Blamed

IT NOW REMAINS to be seen what are the methods and rules for a prince as regards his subjects and friends. And as I know that many have written of this, I fear that my writing about it may be deemed presumptuous, differing as I do, especially in this matter, from the opinions of others. But my intention being to write something of use to those who understand, it appears to me more proper to go to the real truth of the matter than to its imagination; and many have imagined republics and principalities which have never been seen or known to exist in reality; for how we live is so far removed from how we ought to live, that he who abandons what is done for what ought to be done, will rather learn to bring about his own ruin than his preservation. A man who wishes to make a profession of goodness in everything must necessarily come to grief among so many who are not good. Therefore it is necessary for a prince, who wishes to maintain himself, to learn how not to be good, and to use this knowledge and not use it, according to the necessity of the case.

Leaving on one side, then, those things which concern only an imaginary prince, and speaking of those that are real, I state that all men, and especially princes, who are placed at a greater height, are reputed for certain qualities which bring them either praise or blame. Thus one is considered liberal, another *misero* or miserly (using a Tuscan term, seeing that *avaro* with us still means one who is rapaciously acquisitive and *misero* one who makes grudging use of his own) ; one a free giver, another rapacious; one cruel, another merciful;

one a breaker of his word, another trustworthy; one effeminate and pusillanimous, another fierce and high-
spirited; one humane, another haughty; one lascivious,
another chaste; one frank, another astute; one hard,
another easy; one serious, another frivolous; one religious, another an unbeliever, and so on. I know that
every one will admit that it would be highly praise-
worthy in a prince to possess all the above-named qualities that are reputed good, but as they cannot all be
possessed or observed, human conditions not permitting
of it, it is necessary that he should be prudent enough
to avoid the scandal of those vices which would lose
him the state, and guard himself if possible against those
which will not lose it him, but if not able to, he can
indulge them with less scruple. And yet he must not
mind incurring the scandal of those vices, without
which it would be difficult to save the state, for if one
considers well, it will be found that some things which
seem virtues would, if followed, lead to one's ruin, and
some others which appear vices result in one's greater
security and wellbeing.

16

Of Liberality and Niggardliness

BEGINNING NOW with the first qualities above named, I say that it would be well to be considered liberal; nevertheless liberality such as the world understands it will injure you, because if used virtuously and in the proper way, it will not be known, and you will incur the disgrace of the contrary vice. But one who wishes to obtain the reputation of liberality among men, must not omit every kind of sumptuous display, and to such an extent that a prince of this character will consume by such means all his resources, and will be at last compelled, if he wishes to maintain his name for liberality, to impose heavy taxes on his people, become extortionate, and do everything possible to obtain money. This will make his subjects begin to hate him, and he will be little esteemed being poor, so that having by this liberality injured many and benefited but few, he will feel the first little disturbance and be endangered by every peril. If he recognises this and wishes to change his system, he incurs at once the charge of niggardliness.

A prince, therefore, not being able to exercise this virtue of liberality without risk if it be known, must not, if he be prudent, object to be called miserly. In course of time he will be thought more liberal, when it is seen that by his parsimony his revenue is sufficient, that he can defend himself against those who make war on him, and undertake enterprises without burdening his people, so that he is really liberal to all those from whom he does not take, who are infinite in number, and niggardly to all to whom he does not give, who are few. In our times we have seen nothing great done except by those who have been esteemed niggardly; the others have all been ruined. Pope Julius II, although he had made use of a reputation for liberality in order to attain the papacy, did not seek to retain it afterwards, so that he might be able to wage war. The present King of France has carried on so many wars without imposing an extraordinary tax, because his extra expenses were covered by the parsimony he had so long practised. The present King of Spain, if he had been thought liberal, would not have engaged in and been successful in so many enterprises.

For these reasons a prince must care little for the reputation of being a miser, if he wishes to avoid robbing his subjects, if he wishes to be able to defend himself, to avoid becoming poor and contemptible, and not to be forced to become rapacious; this niggardliness is one of those vices which enable him to reign. If it is said that Cæsar attained the empire through liberality, and that many others have reached the highest positions through being liberal or being thought so, I would reply that you are either a prince already or else on the way to become one. In the first case, this liberality is harmful; in the second, it is certainly necessary to be considered liberal. Cæsar was one of those who wished to attain the mastery over Rome, but if after attaining it he had lived and had not moderated his expenses, he would have destroyed that empire. And should any one reply that there have been many princes, who have done great things with their armies, who have been thought extremely liberal, I would answer by saying that the prince may either spend his own wealth and that of his subjects or the wealth of others. In the first case he must be sparing, but for the rest he must not neglect to be very liberal. The liberality is very necessary to a prince who marches with his armies, and lives by plunder, sack and ransom, and is dealing with the wealth of others, for without it he would not be followed by his soldiers. And you may be very generous indeed with what is not the property of yourself or your subjects, as were Cyrus, Cæsar, and Alexander; for spending the

wealth of others will not diminish your reputation, but
increase it, only spending your own resources will injure you. There is nothing which destroys itself so much
as liberality, for by using it you lose the power of using
it, and become either poor and despicable, or, to escape
poverty, rapacious and hated. And of all things that a
prince must guard against, the most important are being
despicable or hated, and liberality will lead you to one
or the other of these conditions. It is, therefore, wiser
to have the name of a miser, which produces disgrace
without hatred, than to incur of necessity the name
of being rapacious, which produces both disgrace and
hatred.

17

Of Cruelty and Clemency, and Whether It Is Better to Be Loved or Feared

PROCEEDING to the other qualities before named, I say that every prince must desire to be considered merciful and not cruel. He must, however, take care not to misuse this mercifulness. Cesare Borgia was considered cruel, but his cruelty had brought order to the Romagna, united it, and reduced it to peace and fealty. If this is considered well, it will be seen that he was really much more merciful than the Florentine people, who, to avoid the name of cruelty, allowed Pistoia to be destroyed. A prince, therefore, must not mind incurring the charge of cruelty for the purpose of keeping his subjects united and faithful; for, with a very few examples, he will be more merciful than those who, from excess of tenderness, allow disorders to arise, from whence spring bloodshed and rapine; for these as a rule injure the whole community, while the executions carried out by the prince injure only individuals. And of all princes, it is impossible for a new prince to escape the reputation of cruelty, new states being always full of dangers. Wherefore Virgil through the mouth of Dido says:

> *Res dura, et regni novitas me talia cogunt*
> *Moliri, et late fines custode tueri.*

Nevertheless, he must be cautious in believing and acting, and must not be afraid of his own shadow, and must proceed in a temperate manner with prudence and humanity, so that too much confidence does not render him incautious, and too much diffidence does not render him intolerant.

From this arises the question whether it is better to

be loved more than feared, or feared more than loved. The reply is, that one ought to be both feared and loved, but as it is difficult for the two to go together, it is much safer to be feared than loved, if one of the two has to be wanting. For it may be said of men in general that they are ungrateful, voluble, dissemblers, anxious to avoid danger, and covetous of gain; as long as you benefit them, they are entirely yours; they offer you their blood, their goods, their life, and their children, as I have before said, when the necessity is remote; but when it approaches, they revolt. And the prince who has relied solely on their words, without making other preparations, is ruined; for the friendship which is gained by purchase and not through grandeur and nobility of spirit is bought but not secured, and at a pinch is not to be expended in your service. And men have less scruple in offending one who makes himself loved than one who makes himself feared; for love is held by a chain of obligation which, men being selfish, is broken whenever it serves their purpose; but fear is maintained by a dread of punishment which never fails.

Still, a prince should make himself feared in such a way that if he does not gain love, he at any rate avoids hatred; for fear and the absence of hatred may well go together, and will be always attained by one who abstains from interfering with the property of his citizens and subjects or with their women. And when he is obliged to take the life of any one, let him do so when there is a proper justification and manifest reason for it; but above all he must abstain from taking the property of others, for men forget more easily the death of their father than the loss of their patrimony. Then also pretexts for seizing property are never wanting, and one who begins to live by rapine will always find some reason for taking the goods of others, whereas causes for taking life are rarer and more fleeting.

But when the prince is with his army and has a large number of soldiers under his control, then it is extremely necessary that he should not mind being thought cruel; for without this reputation he could not

keep an army united or disposed to any duty. Among
the noteworthy actions of Hannibal is numbered this,
that although he had an enormous army, composed of
men of all nations and fighting in foreign countries, there
never arose any dissension either among them or against
the prince, either in good fortune or in bad. This could
not be due to anything but his inhuman cruelty, which
together with his infinite other virtues, made him always
venerated and terrible in the sight of his soldiers, and
without it his other virtues would not have sufficed to
produce that effect. Thoughtless writers admire on the
one hand his actions, and on the other blame the principal cause of them.

And that it is true that his other virtues would not
have sufficed may be seen from the case of Scipio (famous not only in regard to his own times, but all times
of which memory remains), whose armies rebelled against
him in Spain, which arose from nothing but his excessive
kindness, which allowed more licence to the soldiers
than was consonant with military discipline. He was re-
proached with this in the senate by Fabius Maximus,
who called him a corrupter of the Roman militia. Locri
having been destroyed by one of Scipio's officers was not
revenged by him, nor was the insolence of that officer
punished, simply by reason of his easy nature; so much
so, that some one wishing to excuse him in the senate,
said that there were many men who knew rather how
not to err, than how to correct the errors of others. This
disposition would in time have tarnished the fame and
glory of Scipio had he persevered in it under the empire,
but living under the rule of the senate this harmful
quality was not only concealed but became a glory to
him.

I conclude, therefore, with regard to being feared and
loved, that men love at their own free will, but fear
at the will of the prince, and that a wise prince must
rely on what is in his power and not on what is in the
power of others, and he must only contrive to avoid
incurring hatred, as has been explained.

18

In What Way Princes Must Keep Faith

HOW LAUDABLE IT IS for a prince to keep good faith and live with integrity, and not with astuteness, every one knows. Still the experience of our times shows those princes to have done great things who have had little regard for good faith, and have been able by astuteness to confuse men's brains, and who have ultimately overcome those who have made loyalty their foundation.

You must know, then, that there are two methods of fighting, the one by law, the other by force: the first method is that of men, the second of beasts; but as the first method is often insufficient, one must have recourse to the second. It is therefore necessary for a prince to know well how to use both the beast and the man. This was covertly taught to rulers by ancient writers, who relate how Achilles and many others of those ancient princes were given to Chiron the centaur to be brought up and educated under his discipline. The parable of this semi-animal, semi-human teacher is meant to indicate that a prince must know how to use both natures, and that the one without the other is not durable.

A prince being thus obliged to know well how to act as a beast must imitate the fox and the lion, for the lion cannot protect himself from traps, and the fox cannot defend himself from wolves. One must therefore be a fox to recognise traps, and a lion to frighten wolves. Those that wish to be only lions do not understand this. Therefore, a prudent ruler ought not to keep faith when by so doing it would be against his interest, and when the reasons which made him bind himself no longer exist. If men were all good, this precept would not be a good one; but as they are bad, and would not observe their faith with you, so you are not bound to keep faith with them. Nor have legitimate grounds ever failed a prince who wished to show colourable excuse for the non-fulfilment of his promise. Of this one could furnish an infinite number of modern examples, and show how many times peace has been broken, and how many promises rendered worthless, by the faithlessness of princes, and those that have been best able to imitate the fox have succeeded best. But it is necessary to be able to disguise this character well, and to be a great feigner and dissembler; and men are so simple and so ready to obey present necessities, that one who deceives will always find those who allow themselves to be deceived.

I will only mention one modern instance. Alexander VI did nothing else but deceive men, he thought of nothing else, and found the occasion for it; no man was ever more able to give assurances, or affirmed things with stronger oaths, and no man observed them less; however, he always succeeded in his deceptions, as he well knew this aspect of things.

It is not, therefore, necessary for a prince to have all the above-named qualities, but it is very necessary to seem to have them. I would even be bold to say that to possess them and always to observe them is dangerous, but to appear to possess them is useful. Thus it is well to seem merciful, faithful, humane, sincere, religious, and also to be so; but you must have the mind so disposed that when it is needful to be otherwise you may be able to change to the opposite qualities. And it must be understood that a prince, and especially a new prince, cannot observe all those things which are considered good in men, being often obliged, in order to maintain the state, to act against faith, against charity, against humanity, and against religion. And, therefore, he must have a mind disposed to adapt itself according to the wind, and as the variations of fortune dictate, and, as I said before, not deviate from what is good, if possible, but be able to do evil if constrained.

A prince must take great care that nothing goes out of his mouth which is not full of the above-named five qualities, and, to see and hear him, he should seem to be all mercy, faith, integrity, humanity, and religion. And nothing is more necessary than to seem to have this last quality, for men in general judge more by the eyes than by the hands, for every one can see, but very few have to feel. Everybody sees what you appear to be, few feel what you are, and those few will not dare to oppose themselves to the many, who have the majesty of the state to defend them; and in the actions of men, and especially of princes, from which there is no appeal, the end justifies the means. Let a prince therefore aim at conquering and maintaining the state, and the means will always be judged honourable and praised by every one, for the vulgar is always taken by appearances and the issue of the event; and the world consists only of the vulgar, and the few who are not vulgar are isolated when the many have a rallying point in the prince. A certain prince of the present time, whom it is well not to name, never does anything but preach peace and good faith, but he is really a great enemy to both, and either of them, had he observed them, would have lost him state or reputation on many occasions.

19

That We Must Avoid Being Despised and Hated

BUT AS I HAVE NOW SPOKEN of the most important of the qualities in question, I will now deal briefly and generally with the rest. The prince must, as already stated, avoid those things which will make him hated or despised; and whenever he succeeds in this, he will have done his part, and will find no danger in other vices. He will chiefly become hated, as I said, by being rapacious, and usurping the property and women of his subjects, which he must abstain from doing, and whenever one does not attack the property or honour of the generality of men, they will live contented; and one will only have to combat the ambition of a few, who can be easily held in check in many ways. He is rendered despicable by being thought changeable, frivolous, effeminate, timid, and irresolute; which a prince must guard against as a rock of danger, and so contrive that his actions show grandeur, spirit, gravity, and fortitude; and as to the government of his subjects, let his sentence be irrevocable, and let him adhere to his decisions so that no one may think of deceiving or cozening him.

The prince who creates such an opinion of himself gets a great reputation, and it is very difficult to conspire against one who has a great reputation, and he will not easily be attacked, so long as it is known that he is capable and reverenced by his subjects. For a prince must have two kinds of fear: one internal as regards his subjects, one external as regards foreign powers. From the latter he can defend himself with good arms and good friends, and he will always have good friends if he has good arms; and internal matters will

always remain quiet, if they are not perturbed by conspiracy and there is no disturbance from without; and
even if external powers sought to attack him, if he has
ruled and lived as I have described, he will always if
he stands firm, be able to sustain every shock, as I have
shown that Nabis the Spartan did. But with regard
to the subjects, if not acted on from outside, it is still
to be feared lest they conspire in secret, from which the
prince may guard himself well by avoiding hatred and
contempt, and keeping the people satisfied with him,
which it is necessary to accomplish, as has been related
at length. And one of the most potent remedies that a
prince has against conspiracies, is that of not being hated
by the mass of the people; for whoever conspires
always believes that he will satisfy the people by the
death of their prince; but if he thought to offend them
by doing this, he would fear to engage in such an undertaking, for the difficulties that conspirators have
to meet are infinite. Experience shows that there have
been very many conspiracies, but few have turned out
well, for whoever conspires cannot act alone, and cannot
find companions except among those who are discontented; and as soon as you have disclosed your intention
to a malcontent, you give him the means of satisfying himself, for by revealing it he can hope to secure
everything he wants; to such an extent that seeing a
certain gain by doing this, and seeing on the other hand
only a doubtful one and full of danger, he must either
be a rare friend to you or else a very bitter enemy to
the prince if he keeps faith with you. And to express
the matter in a few words, I say, that on the side of the
conspirator there is nothing but fear, jealousy, suspicion, and dread of punishment which frightens him; and
on the side of the prince there is the majesty of government, the laws, the protection of friends and of the
state which guard him. When to these things is added
the goodwill of the people, it is impossible that any one
should have the temerity to conspire. For whereas generally a conspirator has to fear before the execution of
his plot, in this case, having the people for an enemy,

he must also fear after his crime is accomplished, and thus he is not able to hope for any refuge.

Numberless instances might be given of this, but I will content myself with one which took place within the memory of our fathers. Messer Annibale Bentivogli, Prince of Bologna, ancestor of the present Messer Annibale, was killed by the Canneschi, who conspired against him. He left no relations but Messer Giovanni, who was then an infant, but after the murder the people rose up and killed all the Canneschi. This arose from the popular goodwill that the house of Bentivogli enjoyed at that time, which was so great that, as there was nobody left after the death of Annibale who could govern the state, the Bolognese hearing that there was one of the Bentivogli family in Florence, who had till then been thought the son of a blacksmith, came to fetch him and gave him the government of the city, and it was governed by him until Messer Giovanni was old enough to assume the government.

I conclude, therefore, that a prince need trouble little about conspiracies when the people are well disposed, but when they are hostile and hold him in hatred, then he must fear everything and everybody. Well-ordered states and wise princes have studied diligently not to drive the nobles to desperation, and to satisfy the populace and keep it contented, for this is one of the most important matters that a prince has to deal with.

Among the kingdoms that are well ordered and governed in our time is France, and there we find numberless good institutions on which depend the liberty and security of the king; of these the chief is the parliament and its authority, because he who established that kingdom, knowing the ambition and insolence of the great nobles, deemed it necessary to have a bit in their mouths to check them. And knowing on the other hand the hatred of the mass of the people against the great, based on fear, and wishing to secure them, he did not wish to make this the special care of the king, to relieve him of the dissatisfaction that he might incur among the nobles by favouring the people, and among the people by favouring the nobles. He therefore established a third judge that, without direct charge of the king, kept in check the great and favoured the lesser people. Nor could any better or more prudent measure have been adopted, nor better precaution for the safety of the king and the kingdom. From which another notable rule can be drawn, that princes should let the carrying out of unpopular duties devolve on others, and bestow favours themselves. I conclude again by saying that a prince must esteem his nobles, but not make himself hated by the populace.

It may perhaps seem to some, that considering the life and death of many Roman emperors that they are instances contrary to my opinion, finding that some who always lived nobly and showed great strength of character, nevertheless lost the empire, or were killed by their subjects who conspired against them. Wishing to answer these objections, I will discuss the qualities of some emperors, showing the cause of their ruin not to be at variance with what I have stated, and I will also meanwhile consider the things to be noted by whoever reads the deeds of these times. I will content myself with taking all those emperors who succeeded to the empire from Marcus the philosopher to Maximinus; these were Marcus, Commodus his son, Pertinax, Julianus, Severus, Antoninus, Caracalla his son, Macrinus, Heliogabalus, Alexander, and Maximinus. And the first thing to note is, that whereas other princes have only to contend against the ambition of the great and the insolence of the people, the Roman emperors had a third difficulty, that of having to support the cruelty and avarice of the soldiers, which was such that it was the cause of the ruin of many, it being hardly possible to satisfy both the soldiers and the people. For the people love tranquility, and therefore like pacific princes, but the soldiers prefer a prince of military spirit, who is insolent, cruel, and rapacious. They wish him to exercise these qualities on the people so that they may get double pay and give vent to their avarice and cruelty. Thus it came about that those emperors who, by nature or art, had not such a reputation as could keep both parties in check, were invariably ruined, and the greater number of them who were raised to the empire being new men, knowing the difficulties of these two opposite dispositions, confined themselves to satisfying the soldiers, and thought little of injuring the people. This choice was necessary, princes not being able to avoid being hated by some one. They must first try not to be hated by the mass of the people; if they cannot accomplish this they must use every means to escape the hatred of the most powerful parties. And therefore these emperors, who being new men had need of extraordinary favours, adhered to the soldiers rather than to the people; whether this, however, was of use to them or not, depended on whether the prince knew how to maintain his reputation with them. From these causes it resulted that Marcus, Pertinax, and Alexander, being all of modest life, lovers of justice, enemies of cruelty, humane and benign, all came to a sad end except Marcus. Marcus alone lived and died in honour, because he succeeded to the empire by hereditary right and did not owe it either to the soldiers or to the people; besides which, possessing many virtues which made him revered, he kept both parties in their place as long as he lived and was never either hated or despised. But Pertinax was created emperor against the will of the soldiers, who being accustomed to live licentiously under Commodus, could not put up with the honest life to which Pertinax wished to limit them, so that having made himself hated, and to this contempt being added because he was old, he was ruined at the very beginning of his administration.

Whence it may be seen that hatred is gained as much by good works as by evil, and therefore, as I said before, a prince who wishes to maintain the state is often forced to do evil, for when that party, whether populace, soldiery, or nobles, whichever it be that you consider necessary to you for keeping your position, is corrupt, you must follow its humour and satisfy it, and in that case good works will be inimical to you.

But let us come to Alexander, who was of such goodness, that among other things for which he is praised, it is said that in the fourteen years that he reigned no one was put to death by him without a fair trial. Nevertheless, being considered effeminate, and a man who allowed himself to be ruled by his mother, and having thus fallen into contempt, the army conspired against him and killed him.

Considering, on the other hand, the qualities of Commodus, Severus, Antoninus, Caracalla, and Maximinus, you will find them extremely cruel and rapacious; to satisfy the soldiers there was no injury which they would not inflict on the people, and all except Severus ended badly. Severus, however, had such abilities that by maintaining the soldiers friendly to him, he was able to reign happily, although he oppressed the people, for his virtues made him so admirable in the sight both of the soldiers and the people that the latter were, in some degree, astonished and stupefied, while the former were respectful and contented.

As the deeds of this ruler were great and notable for a new prince, I will briefly show how well he could use the qualities of the fox and the lion, whose natures, as I said before, it is necessary for a prince to imitate. Knowing the sloth of the Emperor Julianus, Severus, who was leader of the army in Slavonia, persuaded the troops that it would be well to go to Rome to avenge the death of Pertinax, who had been slain by the Prætorian guard, and under this pretext, without revealing his aspirations to the throne, marched with his army to Rome and was in Italy before his departure was known. On his arrival in Rome the senate elected him emperor through fear, and killed Julianus. There remained after this beginning two difficulties to be faced by Severus before he could obtain the whole control of the empire: one in Asia, where Nigrinus, head of the Asiatic armies, had declared himself emperor; the other in the west from Albinus, who also aspired to the empire. And as he judged it dangerous to show himself hostile to both, he decided to attack Nigrinus and deceive Albinus, to

whom he wrote that having been elected emperor by
the senate he wished to share that dignity with him;
he sent him the title of Cæsar and, by deliberation of
the senate, he was declared his colleague; all of which
was accepted as true by Albinus. But when Severus
had defeated and killed Nigrinus, and pacified things in
the East, he returned to Rome and charged Albinus in
the senate with having, unmindful of the benefits received from him, traitorously sought to assassinate him,
and stated that he was therefore obliged to go and
punish his ingratitude. He then went to France to meet
him, and there deprived him of both his position and
his life.

Whoever examines in detail the actions of Severus,
will find him to have been a very ferocious lion and an
extremely astute fox, and will find him to have been
feared and respected by all and not hated by the army;
and will not be surprised that he, a new man, should
have been able to hold so much power, since his great
reputation defended him always from the hatred that
his rapacity might have produced in the people. But
Antoninus his son was also a man of great ability, and
possessed qualities that rendered him admirable in the
sight of the people and also made him popular with
the soldiers, for he was a military man, capable of enduring the most extreme hardships, disdainful of deli-
cate food, and every other luxury, which made him
loved by all the armies. However, his ferocity and
cruelty were so great and unheard of, through his having, after executing many private individuals, caused
a large part of the population of Rome and all that of
Alexandria to be killed, that he became hated by all
the world and began to be feared by those about him
to such an extent that he was finally killed by a centurion in the midst of his army. Whence it is to be noted
that this kind of death, which proceeds from the deliberate action of a determined man, cannnot be avoided by
princes, since any one who does not fear death himself
can inflict it, but a prince need not fear much on this
account, as such men are extremely rare. He must only

guard against committing any grave injury to any one
he makes use of, or has about him for his service, like
Antoninus had done, having caused the death with con-
tumely of the brother of that centurion, and also threat-
ened him every day, although he still retained him in his
bodyguard, which was a foolish and dangerous thing
to do, as the fact proved.

But let us come to Commodus, who might easily have
kept the empire, having succeeded to it by heredity, being the son of Marcus, and it would have sufficed for
him to follow in the steps of his father to have satisfied
both the people and the soldiers. But being of a cruel
and bestial disposition, in order to be able to exercise
his rapacity on the people, he sought to favour the
soldiers and render them licentious; on the other hand,
by not maintaining his dignity, by often descending into the theatre to fight with gladiators and committing
other contemptible actions, little worthy of the imperial
dignity, he became despicable in the eyes of the soldiers,
and being hated on the one hand and despised on the
other, he was conspired against and killed.

There remains to be described the character of Maximinus. He was an extremely warlike man, and as the
armies were annoyed with the effeminacy of Alexander,
which we have already spoken of, he was elected emperor
after the death of the latter. He did not enjoy it for long,
as two things made him hated and despised: the one his
base origin, as he had been a shepherd in Thrace, which
was generally known and caused great disdain on all
sides; the other, because he had at the commencement
of his rule deferred going to Rome to take possession of
the Imperial seat, and had obtained a reputation for
great cruelty, having through his prefects in Rome and
other parts of the empire committed many acts of cruelty.
The whole world being thus moved by indignation for
the baseness of his blood, and also by the hatred caused
by fear of his ferocity, he was conspired against first by
Africa and afterwards by the senate and all the people
of Rome and Italy. His own army also joined them, for
besieging Aquileia and finding it difficult to take, they

became enraged at his cruelty, and seeing that he had so many enemies, they feared him less and put him to death.

I will not speak of Heliogabalus, of Macrinus, or Julianus, who being entirely contemptible were immediately suppressed, but I will come to the conclusion of this discourse by saying that the princes of our time have less difficulty than these in being obliged to satisfy in an extraordinary degree their soldiers in their states; for although they must have a certain consideration for them, yet any difficulty is soon settled, for none of these princes have armies that are inextricably bound up with the administration of the government and the rule of their provinces as were the armies of the Roman empire. If it was then necessary to satisfy the soldiers rather than the people, it was because the soldiers could do more than the people; now, it is more necessary for all princes, except the Turk and the Sultan, to satisfy the people than the soldiers, for the people can do more than the soldiers. I except the Turk, because he always keeps about him twelve thousand infantry and fifteen thousand cavalry, on which depend the security and strength of his kingdom; and it is necessary for him to postpone every other consideration to keep them friendly. It is the same with the kingdom of the Sultan, which being entirely in the hands of the soldiers, he is bound to keep their friendship regardless of the people. And it is to be noted that this state of the Sultan is different from that of all other princes, being similar to the Christian pontificate, which cannot be called either a hereditary kingdom or a new one, for the sons of the dead prince are not his heirs, but he who is elected to that position by those who have authority. And as this order is ancient it cannot be called a new kingdom, there being none of these difficulties which exist in new ones; as although the prince is new, the rules of that state are old and arranged to receive him as if he were their hereditary lord.

But returning to our matter, I say that whoever studies the preceding argument will see that either hatred or contempt were the causes of the ruin of the emperors

named, and will also observe how it came about that,
some of them acting in one way and some in another, in
both ways there were some who had a fortunate and
others an unfortunate ending. As Pertinax and Alexander were both new rulers, it was useless and injurious
for them to try and imitate Marcus, who was a hereditary
prince; and similarly with Caracalla, Commodus, and
Maximinus it was pernicious for them to imitate Severus,
as they had not sufficient ability to follow in his footsteps.
Thus a new prince cannot imitate the actions of Marcus,
in his dominions, nor is it necessary for him to imitate
those of Severus; but he must take from Severus those
things that are necessary to found his state, and from
Marcus those that are useful and glorious for conserving
a state that is already established and secure.

20

Whether Fortresses and Other Things Which Princes Often Contrive Are Useful or Injurious

SOME PRINCES, in order to hold their possessions securely, have disarmed their citizens, some others have kept their subject lands divided into parts, others have fomented enmities against themselves, others have endeavoured to win over those whom they suspected at the commencement of their rule: some have constructed fortresses, others have cast them down and destroyed them. And although one cannot pronounce a definite judgment as to these things without going into the particulars of the state to which such a deliberation is to be applied, still I will speak in such a general way as the matter will permit.

A new prince has never been known to disarm his subjects, on the contrary, when he has found them disarmed he has always armed them, for by arming them these arms become your own, those that you suspected become faithful and those that were faithful remain so, and from being merely subjects become your partisans. And since all the subjects cannot be armed, when you give the privilege of arms to some, you can deal more safely with the others; and this different treatment that they recognize renders your men more obliged to you. The others will excuse you, judging that those have necessarily greater merit who have greater danger and heavier duties. But when you disarm them, you commence to offend them and show that you distrust them either through cowardice or lack of confidence, and both of these opinions generate hatred against you. And as you cannot remain unarmed, you are obliged to resort to a mercenary militia, of which we have already stated the value; and even if it were good it cannot be sufficient in number to defend you against powerful enemies and suspected subjects. Therefore, as I have said, a new prince in a new dominion always has his subjects armed. History is full of such examples.

But when a prince acquires a new state as an addition to his old one, then it is necessary to disarm that state, except those who in acquiring it have sided with you; and even these one must, when time and opportunity serve, render weak and effeminate, and arrange things so that all the arms of the new state are in the hands of your soldiers who live near you in your old state.

Our forefathers and those who were esteemed wise used to say that it was necessary to hold Pistoia by means of factions and Pisa with fortresses, and for this purpose they fomented differences in some of their subject towns in order to possess them more easily. In those days when there was a balance of power in Italy, this was doubtless well done, but does not seem to me to be a good precept for the present time, for I do not believe that the divisions thus created ever do any good; on the contrary it is certain that when the enemy approaches, the cities thus divided will be at once lost, for the weaker faction will always side with the enemy and the other will not be able to stand.

The Venetians, actuated, I believe, by the aforesaid motives, fomented the Guelf and Ghibelline factions in the cities subject to them, and although they never allowed them to come to bloodshed, they yet encouraged these differences among them, so that the citizens, being occupied in their own quarrels, might not act against them. This, however, did not avail them anything, as was seen when, after the defeat of Vailà, a part of those subjects immediately took courage and seized the whole state. Such methods, besides, argue weakness in a prince, for in a strong government such dissensions will never be permitted. They are profitable only in time of peace, as by such means it is easy to manage one's subjects, but when it comes to war, the fallacy of such a policy is at once shown.

Without doubt princes become great when they overcome difficulties and opposition, and therefore fortune, especially when it wants to render a new prince great, who has greater need of gaining a great reputation than a hereditary prince, raises up enemies and compels him to undertake wars against them, so that he may have cause to overcome them, and thus climb up higher by means of that ladder which his enemies have brought him. There are many who think therefore that a wise prince ought, when he has the chance, to foment astutely some enmity, so that by suppressing it he will augment his greatness.

Princes, and especially new ones, have found more faith and more usefulness in those men, whom at the beginning of their power they regarded with suspicion, than in those they at first confided in. Pandolfo Petrucci, Prince of Siena, governed his state more by those whom he suspected than by others. But of this we cannot speak at large, as it strays from the subject; I will merely say that these men who at the beginning of a new government were enemies, if they are of a kind to need support to maintain their position, can be very easily gained by the prince, and they are the more compelled to serve him faithfully as they know they must by their deeds cancel the bad opinion previously held of them, and thus the prince will always derive greater help from them than from those who, serving him with greater security, neglect his interests.

And as the matter requires it, I will not omit to remind a prince who has newly taken a state with the secret help of its inhabitants, that he must consider well the motives that have induced those who have favoured him to do so, and if it is not natural affection for him but only because they were not contented with the state as it was, he will have great trouble and difficulty in maintaining their friendship, because it will be impossible for him to content them. And on well examining the cause of this in the examples drawn from ancient and modern times it will be seen that it is much easier to gain the friendship of those men who were contented with the previous condition and were therefore at first enemies, than that of those who not being contented, became his friends and helped him to occupy it.

It has been the custom of princes in order to be able to hold their state securely, to erect fortresses, as a bridle and bit to those who have designs against them, and in order to have a secure refuge against a sudden assault. I approve this method, because it was anciently used. Nevertheless, Messer Niccolò Vitelli has been seen in our own time to destroy two fortresses in Città di Castello in order to keep that state. Guid'Ubaldo, Duke of Urbino, on returning to his dominions from which he had been driven by Cesare Borgia, razed to their foundations all the fortresses of that province, and considered that without them it would be more difficult for him to lose the state again. The Bentivogli, in returning to Bologna, took similar measures. Therefore fortresses may or may not be useful according to the times; if they do good in one way, they do harm in another. The question may be discussed thus: a prince who fears his own people more than foreigners ought to build fortresses, but he who has greater fear of foreigners than of his own people ought to do without them. The castle of Milan built by Francesco Sforza has given and will give more trouble to the house of Sforza than any other disorder in that state. Therefore the best fortress is to be found in the love of the people, for although you may have fortresses they will not save you if you are hated by the people. When once the people have taken arms against you, there will never be lacking foreigners to assist them. In our times we do not see that they have profited any ruler, except the Countess of Forlì on the death of her consort Count Girolamo, for she was thus enabled to escape the popular rising and await help from Milan and recover the state; the circumstances being then such that no foreigner could assist the people. But afterwards they were of little use to her when Cesare Borgia attacked her and the people being hostile to her allied themselves with the foreigner. So that then and before it would have been safer for her not to have been hated by the people than to have had the fortresses. Having considered these things I would therefore praise the one who erects fortresses and the one who does not, and would blame any one who, trusting in them, recks little of being hated by his people.

21

How a Prince Must Act in Order to Gain Reputation

NOTHING CAUSES a prince to be so much esteemed as great enterprises and giving proof of prowess. We have in our own day Ferdinand, King of Aragon, the present King of Spain. He may almost be termed a new prince, because from a weak king he has become for fame and glory the first king in Christendom, and if you regard his actions you will find them all very great and some of them extraordinary. At the very beginning of his reign he assailed Granada, and that enterprise was the foundation of his state. At first he did it at his leisure and without fear of being interfered with; he kept the minds of the barons of Castile occupied in this enterprise, so that thinking only of that war they did not think of making innovations, and he thus acquired reputation and power over them without their being aware of it. He was able with the money of the Church and the people to maintain his armies, and by that long war to lay the foundations of his military power, which afterwards has made him famous. Besides this, to be able to undertake greater enterprises, and always under the pretext of religion, he had recourse to a pious cruelty, driving out the Moors from his kingdom and despoiling them. No more miserable or unusual example can be found. He also attacked Africa under the same pretext, undertook his Italian enterprise, and has lately attacked France; so that he has continually contrived great things, which have kept his subjects' minds uncertain and astonished, and occupied in watching their results. And these actions have arisen one out of the other, so that they have left no time for men to settle down and act against him.

It is also very profitable for a prince to give some outstanding example of his greatness in the internal administration, like those related of Messer Bernabò of Milan. When it happens that some one does something extraordinary, either good or evil, in civil life, he must find such means of rewarding or punishing him which will be much talked about. And above all a prince must endeavour in every action to obtain fame for being great and excellent.

A prince is further esteemed when he is a true friend or a true enemy, when, that is, he declares himself without reserve in favour of some one or against another. This policy is always more useful than remaining neutral. For if two neighbouring powers come to blows, they are either such that if one wins, you will have to fear the victor, or else not. In either of these two cases it will be better for you to declare yourself openly and make war, because in the first case if you do not declare yourself, you will fall a prey to the victor, to the pleasure and satisfaction of the one who has been defeated, and you will have no reason nor anything to defend you and nobody to receive you. For, whoever wins will not desire friends whom he suspects and who do not help him when in trouble, and whoever loses will not receive you as you did not take up arms to venture yourself in his cause.

Antiochus went to Greece, being sent by the Ætolians to expel the Romans. He sent orators to the Achaeans who were friends of the Romans to encourage them to remain neutral; on the other hand the Romans persuaded them to take up arms on their side. The matter was brought before the council of the Achaeans for deliberation, where the ambassador of Antiochus sought to persuade them to remain neutral, to which the Roman ambassador replied: "As to what is said that it is best and most useful for your state not to meddle in our war, nothing is further from the truth; for if you do not meddle in it you will become, without any favour or any reputation, the prize of the victor."

And it will always happen that the one who is not your friend will want you to remain neutral, and the

one who is your friend will require you to declare yourself by taking arms. Irresolute princes, to avoid present
dangers, usually follow the way of neutrality and are
mostly ruined by it. But when the prince declares himself frankly in favour of one side, if the one to whom
you adhere conquers, even if he is powerful and you
remain at his discretion, he is under an obligation to
you and friendship has been established, and men are
never so dishonest as to oppress you with such a patent
ingratitude. Moreover, victories are never so prosper-
ous that the victor does not need to have some scruples,
especially as to justice. But if your ally loses, you are
sheltered by him, and so long as he can, he will assist
you; you become the companion of a fortune which may
rise again. In the second case, when those who fight are
such that you have nothing to fear from the victor, it
is still more prudent on your part to adhere to one; for
you go to the ruin of one with the help of him who
ought to save him if he were wise, and if he conquers
he rests at your discretion, and it is impossible that he
should not conquer with your help.

And here it should be noted that a prince ought never
to make common cause with one more powerful than
himself to injure another, unless necessity forces him to
it, as before said; for if he wins you rest in his power,
and princes must avoid as much as possible being under
the will and pleasure of others. The Venetians united
with France against the Duke of Milan, although they
could have avoided that alliance, and from it resulted
their own ruin. But when one cannot avoid it, as happened in the case of the Florentines when the Pope and
Spain went with their armies to attack Lombardy, then
the prince ought to join for the above reasons. Let no
state believe that it can always follow a safe policy, rather
let it think that all are doubtful. This is found in the
nature of things, that one never tries to avoid one difficulty without running into another, but prudence consists
in being able to know the nature of the difficulties, and
taking the least harmful as good.

A prince must also show himself a lover of merit, give

preferment to the able, and honour those who excel in every art. Moreover he must encourage his citizens to follow their callings quietly, whether in commerce, or agriculture, or any other trade that men follow, so that this one shall not refrain from improving his possessions through fear that they may be taken from him, and that one from starting a trade for fear of taxes; but he should offer rewards to whoever does these things, and to whoever seeks in any way to improve his city or state. Besides this, he ought, at convenient seasons of the year, to keep the people occupied with festivals and shows; and as every city is divided either into guilds or into classes, he ought to pay attention to all these groups, mingle with them from time to time, and give them an example of his humanity and munificence, always upholding, however, the majesty of his dignity, which must never be allowed to fail in anything whatever.

22

Of the Secretaries of Princes

THE CHOICE of a prince's ministers is a matter of no little importance; they are either good or not according to the prudence of the prince. The first impression that one gets of a ruler and of his brains is from seeing the men that he has about him. When they are competent and faithful one can always consider him wise, as he has been able to recognise their ability and keep them faithful. But when they are the reverse, one can always form an unfavourable opinion of him, because the first mistake that he makes is in making this choice.

There was nobody who knew Messer Antonio da Venafro as the minister of Pandolfo Petrucci, Prince of Siena, who did not consider Pandolfo to be a very prudent man, having him for his minister. There are three different kinds of brains, the one understands things unassisted, the other understands things when shown by others, the third understands neither alone nor with the explanations of others. The first kind is most excellent, the second also excellent, but the third useless. It is therefore evident that if Pandolfo was not of the first kind, he was at any rate of the second. For every time the prince has the judgment to know the good and evil that anyone does or says, even if he has no originality of intellect, yet he can recognise the bad and good works of his minister and correct the one and encourage the other; and the minister cannot hope to deceive him and therefore remains good.

For a prince to be able to know a minister there is this method which never fails. When you see the minister think more of himself than of you, and in all his actions seek his own profit, such a man will never be a good minister, and you can never rely on him; for whoever has in hand the state of another must never think of himself but of the prince, and not mind anything but what relates to him. And, on the other hand, the prince, in order to retain his fidelity ought to think of his minister, honouring and enriching him, doing him kindnesses, and conferring on him honours and giving him responsible tasks, so that the great honours and riches bestowed on him cause him not to desire other honours and riches, and the offices he holds make him fearful of changes. When princes and their ministers stand in this relation to each other, they can rely the one upon the other; when it is otherwise, the result is always injurious either for one or the other of them.

23

How Flatterers Must Be Shunned

I MUST NOT OMIT an important subject, and mention of a mistake which princes can with difficulty avoid, if they are not very prudent, or if they do not make a good choice. And this is with regard to flatterers, of which courts are full, because men take pleasure in their own things and deceive themselves about them that they can with difficulty guard against this plague; and by wishing to guard against it they run the risk of becoming contemptible. Because there is no other way of guarding one's self against flattery than by letting men understand that they will not offend you by speaking the truth; but when every one can tell you the truth, you lose their respect. A prudent prince must therefore take a third course, by choosing for his council wise men, and giving these alone full liberty to speak the truth to him, but only of those things that he asks and of nothing else; but he must ask them about everything and hear their opinion, and afterwards deliberate by himself in his own way, and in these councils and with each of these men comport himself so that every one may see that the more freely he speaks, the more he will be acceptable. Beyond these he should listen to no one, go about the matter deliberately, and be determined in his decisions. Whoever acts otherwise either acts precipitately through flattery or else changes often through the variety of opinions, from which it follows that he will be little esteemed.

I will give a modern instance of this. Pre' Luca, a follower of Maximilian, the present emperor, speaking of his majesty said that he never took counsel with anybody, and yet that he never did anything as he wished; this arose from his following the contrary method to the aforesaid. As the emperor is a secret man he does not communicate his designs to any one or take any advice, but as on putting them into effect they begin to be known and discovered, they begin to be opposed by those he has about him, and he is easily diverted from his purpose. Hence it comes to pass that what he does one day he undoes the next, no one ever understands what he wishes or intends to do, and no reliance is to be placed on his deliberations.

A prince, therefore, ought always to take counsel, but only when he wishes, not when others wish; on the contrary he ought to discourage absolutely attempts to advise him unless he asks it, but he ought to be a great asker, and a patient hearer of the truth about those things of which he has inquired; indeed, if he finds that any one has scruples in telling him the truth he should be angry. And since some think that a prince who gains the reputation of being prudent is so considered, not by his nature but by the good counsellors he has about him, they are undoubtedly deceived. It is an infallible rule that a prince who is not wise himself cannot be well advised, unless by chance he leaves himself entirely in the hands of one man who rules him in everything, but happens to be a very prudent man. In this case he may doubtless be well governed, but it would not last long, for that governor would in a short time deprive him of the state; but by taking counsel with many, a prince who is not wise will never have united councils and will not be able to bring them to unanimity for himself. The counsellors will all think of their own interests, and he will be unable either to correct or to understand them. And it cannot be otherwise, for men will always be false to you unless they are compelled by necessity to be true. Therefore it must be concluded that wise counsels, from whoever they come, must necessarily be due to the prudence of the prince, and not the prudence of the prince to the good counsels received.

24

Why the Princes of Italy Have Lost Their States

THE BEFORE-MENTIONED THINGS, if prudently observed, make a new prince seem ancient, and render him at once more secure and firmer in the state than if he had been established there of old. For a new prince is much more observed in his actions than a hereditary one, and when these are recognised as virtuous, he wins over men more and they are more bound to him than if he were of the ancient blood. For men are much more taken by present than by past things, and when they find themselves well off in the present, they enjoy it and seek nothing more; on the contrary, they will do all they can to defend him, so long as the prince is not in other things deficient. And thus he will have the double glory of having founded a new realm and adorned it and fortified it with good laws, good arms, good friends and good examples; as he will have double shame who is born a prince and through want of prudence has lost his throne.

And if one considers those rulers who have lost their position in Italy in our days, such as the King of Naples, the Duke of Milan and others, one will find in them first a common defect as to their arms, for the reasons discussed at length, then we observe that some of them either had the people hostile to them, or that if the people were friendly they were not able to make sure of the nobility, for without these defects, states are not lost that have enough strength to be able to keep an army in the field. Philip of Macedon, not the father of Alexander the Great, but the one who was conquered by Titus Quintius, did not possess a great state compared to the greatness of Rome and Greece which assailed him, but being a military man and one who knew how to ingratiate himself with the people and make sure of the great, he was able to sustain the war against them for many years; and if at length he lost his power over some cities, he was still able to keep his kingdom.

Therefore, those of our princes who had held their possessions for many years must not accuse fortune for having lost them, but rather their own remissness; for having never in quiet times considered that things might change (as it is a common fault of men not to reckon on storms in fair weather) when adverse times came, they only thought of fleeing, instead of defending themselves. and hoped that the people, enraged by the insolence of the conquerors, would recall them. This measure, when others are wanting, is good; but it is very bad to have neglected the other remedies for that one, for nobody would desire to fall because he believed that he would then find some one to pick him up. This may or may not take place, and if it does, it does not afford you security, as you have not helped yourself but been helped like a coward. Only those defences are good, certain and durable, which depend on yourself alone and your own ability.

25

How Much Fortune Can Do in Human Affairs and How It May Be Opposed

It is not unknown to me how many have been and are of opinion that worldly events are so governed by fortune and by God, that men cannot by their prudence change them, and that on the contrary there is no remedy whatever, and for this they may judge it to be useless to toil much about them, but let things be ruled by chance. This opinion has been more held in our day, from the great changes that have been seen, and are daily seen, beyond every human conjecture. When I think about them, at times I am partly inclined to share this opinion. Nevertheless, that our free will may not be altogether extinguished, I think it may be true that fortune is the ruler of half our actions, but that she allows the other half or thereabouts to be governed by us. I would compare her to an impetuous river that, when turbulent, inundates the plains, casts down trees and buildings, removes earth from this side and places it on the other; every one flees before it, and everything yields to its fury without being able to oppose it; and yet though it is of such a kind, still when it is quiet, men can make provisions against it by dykes and banks, so that when it rises it will either go into a canal or its rush will not be so wild and dangerous. So it is with fortune, which shows her power where no measures have been taken to resist her, and directs her fury where she knows that no dykes or barriers have been made to hold her. And if you regard Italy, which has been the seat of these changes, and which has given the impulse to them, you will see her to be a country without dykes or banks of any kind. If she had been protected by proper measures, like Germany, Spain, and France, this inundation would not have caused the great changes that it has, or would not have happened at all.

This must suffice as regards opposition to fortune in general. But limiting myself more to particular cases, I would point out how one sees a certain prince to-day fortunate and to-morrow ruined, without seeing that he has changed in character or otherwise. I believe this arises in the first place from the causes that we have already discussed at length; that is to say, because the prince who bases himself entirely on fortune is ruined when fortune changes. I also believe that he is happy whose mode of procedure accords with the needs of the times, and similarly he is unfortunate whose mode of procedure is opposed to the times. For one sees that men in those things which lead them to the aim that each one has in view, namely, glory and riches, proceed in various ways; one with circumspection, another with impetuosity, one by violence, another by cunning, one with patience, another with the reverse; and each by these diverse ways may arrive at his aim. One sees also two cautious men, one of whom succeeds in his designs, and the other not, and in the same way two men succeed equally by different methods, one being cautious, the other impetuous, which arises only from the nature of the times, which does or does not conform to their method of procedure. From this it results, as I have said, that two men, acting differently, attain the same effect, and of two others acting in the same way, one attains his goal and not the other. On this depend also the changes in prosperity, for if it happens that time and circumstances are favourable to one who acts with caution and prudence he will be successful, but if time and circumstances change he will be ruined, because he does not change his mode of procedure. No man is found so prudent as to be able to adapt himself to this, either because he cannot deviate from that to which his nature disposes him, or else because having always prospered by walking in one path, he

cannot persuade himself that it is well to leave it; and
therefore the cautious man, when it is time to act suddenly, does not know how to do so and is consequently
ruined; for if one could change one's nature with time
and circumstances, fortune would never change.

Pope Julius II acted impetuously in everything he did
and found the times and conditions so in conformity
with that mode of procedure, that he always obtained
a good result. Consider the first war that he made
against Bologna while Messer Giovanni Bentivogli was
still living. The Venetians were not pleased with it,
neither was the King of Spain, France was conferring
with him over the enterprise, notwithstanding which,
owing to his fierce and impetuous disposition, he engaged
personally in the expedition. This move caused both
Spain and the Venetians to halt and hesitate, the latter
through fear, the former through the desire to recover
the entire kingdom of Naples. On the other hand, he
engaged with him the King of France, because seeing
him make this move and desiring his friendship in order
to put down the Venetians, that king judged that he
could not refuse him his troops without manifest injury.
Thus Julius by his impetuous move achieved what no
other pontiff with the utmost human prudence would
have succeeded in doing, because, if he had waited till
all arrangements had been made and everything settled
before leaving Rome, as any other pontiff would have
done, it would never have succeeded. For the king of
France would have found a thousand excuses, and the
others would have inspired him with a thousand fears.
I will omit his other actions, which were all of this kind
and which all succeeded well, and the shortness of his
life did not suffer him to experience the contrary, for
had times followed in which it was necessary to act with
caution, his ruin would have resulted, for he would never
have deviated from these methods to which his nature
disposed him.

I conclude then that fortune varying and men remaining fixed in their ways, they are successful so long

as these ways conform to circumstances, but when they are opposed then they are unsuccessful. I certainly think that it is better to be impetuous than cautious, for fortune is a woman, and it is necessary, if you wish to master her, to conquer her by force; and it can be seen that she lets herself be overcome by the bold rather than by those who proceed coldly. And therefore, like a woman, she is always a friend to the young, because they are less cautious, fiercer, and master her with greater audacity.

26

Exhortation to Liberate Italy from the Barbarians

HAVING NOW CONSIDERED all the things we have spoken of, and thought within myself whether at present the time was not propitious in Italy for a new prince, and if there was not a state of things which offered an opportunity to a prudent and capable man to introduce a new system that would do honour to himself and good to the mass of the people, it seems to me that so many things concur to favour a new ruler that I do not know of any time more fitting for such an enterprise. And if, as I said, it was necessary in order that the power of Moses should be displayed, that the people of Israel should be slaves in Egypt, and to give scope for the greatness and courage of Cyrus that the Persians should be oppressed by the Medes, and to illustrate the pre-eminence of Theseus that the Athenians should be dispersed, so at the present time, in order that the might of an Italian genius might be recognised, it was necessary that Italy should be reduced to her present condition, and that she should be more enslaved than the Hebrews, more oppressed than the Persians, and more scattered than the Athenians; without a head, without order, beaten, despoiled, lacerated, and overrun, and that she should have suffered ruin of every kind.

And although before now a gleam of hope has appeared which gave hope that some individual might be appointed by God for her redemption, yet at the highest summit of his career he was thrown aside by fortune, so that now, almost lifeless, she awaits one who may heal her wounds and put a stop to the pillaging of Lombardy, to the rapacity and extortion in the Kingdom of Naples and in Tuscany, and cure her of those sores which have long been festering. Behold how she prays God to send some one to redeem her from this barbarous cruelty and insolence. Behold her ready and willing to follow any standard if only there be some one to raise it. There is nothing now she can hope for but that your illustrious house may place itself at the head of this redemption, being by its power and fortune so exalted, and being favoured by God and the Church, of which it is now the ruler. Nor will this be very difficult, if you call to mind the actions and lives of the men I have named. And although those men were rare and marvellous, they were none the less men, and each of them had less opportunity than the present, for their enterprise was not juster than this, nor easier, nor was God more their friend than He is yours. Here is a just cause; *iustum enim est bellum quibus necessarium, et pia arma ubi nulla nisi in armis spes est.* Here is the greatest willingness, nor can there be great difficulty where there is great willingness, provided that the measures are adopted of those whom I have set before you as examples. Besides this, unexampled wonders have been seen here performed by God, the sea has been opened, a cloud has shown you the road, the rock has given forth water, manna has rained, and everything has contributed to your greatness, the remainder must be done by you. God will not do everything, in order not to deprive us of free will and the portion of the glory that falls to our lot.

It is no marvel that none of the before-mentioned Italians have done that which it is to be hoped your illustrious house may do; and if in so many revolutions in Italy and so many war-like operations, it always seems as if military capacity were extinct, this is because the ancient methods were not good, and no one has arisen who knew how to discover new ones. Nothing does so much honour to a newly-risen man than the new laws and measures which he introduces. These things, when they are well based and have greatness in them, render him revered and admired, and there is not lacking scope in Italy for the introduction of every kind of new or-

ganisation. Here there is a great virtue in the members,
if it were not wanting in the heads. Look how in duels
and in contests of a few the Italians are superior in
strength, dexterity, and intelligence. But when it comes
to armies they make a poor show; which proceeds entirely
from the weakness of the leaders, for those that know
are not obeyed, and every one thinks that he knows,
there being hitherto nobody who has raised himself so
high both by valour and fortune as to make the others
yield. Hence it comes about that for so long a time, in
all the wars waged during the last twenty years, whenever there has been an entirely Italian army it has always
been a failure, as witness Taro, then Alexandria, Capua,
Genoa, Vailà, Bologna, and Mestri.

If your illustrious house, therefore, wishes to follow
those great men who redeemed their countries, it is before all things necessary, as the true foundation of every
undertaking, to provide yourself with your own forces,
for you cannot have more faithful, or truer and better
soldiers. And although each one of them may be good,
they will united become even better when they see themselves commanded by their prince, and honoured and
favoured by him. It is therefore necessary to prepare such
forces in order to be able with Italian prowess to defend
the country from foreigners. And although both the Swiss
and Spanish infantry are deemed terrible, none the less
they each have their defects, so that a third method of
array might not only oppose them, but be confident of
overcoming them. For the Spaniards cannot sustain the
attack of cavalry, and the Swiss have to fear infantry
which meets them with resolution equal to their own.
From which it has resulted, as will be seen by experience,
that the Spaniards cannot sustain the attack of French
cavalry, and the Swiss are overthrown by Spanish infantry. And although a complete example of the latter has
not been seen, yet an instance was furnished in the battle
of Ravenna, where the Spanish infantry attacked the
German battalions, which are organised in the same way
as the Swiss. The Spaniards, through their bodily agility
and aided by their bucklers, had entered between and

under their pikes and were in a position to attack them
safely without the Germans being able to defend themselves; and if the cavalry had not charged them they
would have utterly destroyed them. Knowing therefore
the defects of both these kinds of infantry, a third kind
can be created which can resist cavalry and need not
fear infantry, and this will be done by the choice of arms
and a new organisation. And these are the things which,
when newly introduced, give reputation and grandeur
to a new prince.

This opportunity must not, therefore, be allowed to
pass, so that Italy may at length find her liberator. I
cannot express the love with which he would be received
in all those provinces which have suffered under these
foreign invasions, with what thirst for vengeance, with
what steadfast faith, with what love, with what grateful
tears. What doors would be closed against him? What
people would refuse him obedience? What envy could
oppose him? What Italian would withhold allegiance?
This barbarous domination stinks in the nostrils of every
one. May your illustrious house therefore assume this
task with that courage and those hopes which are inspired
by a just cause, so that under its banner our fatherland
may be raised up, and under its auspices be verified that
saying of Petrarch:

Valour against fell wrath
Will take up arms; and be the combat quickly sped!
For, sure, the ancient worth,
That in Italians stirs the heart, is not yet dead.

Early European History from MENTOR and SIGNET CLASSIC

(0451)

☐ **THE MEDIEVAL WORLD: Europe 1000–1350 by Friedrich Heer.** Translated by Janet Sondheimer. A vivid picture of medieval society stressing the intellectual, creative, religious and political life. "Packed with learning which would burst at the seams were it not controlled by the disciplined order and arranging . . ."—*The New York Times*
(625420—$5.95)

☐ **THE PRINCE by Niccolo Machiavelli.** Translated by Luigi Ricci and with an Introduction by Christian Gauss. Relates Machiavelli's 15th century masterpiece to the political and scholarly developments within the past hundred years. (621239—$1.50)

☐ **THE TRAVELS OF MARCO POLO edited and with an Introduction by Milton Rugoff.** Marco Polo's own classic account of his epic adventures in the Far East. This completely annotated edition is an amalgam of the famous Marsden-Wright translation, edited against other versions for conciseness and clarity. (517172—$3.50)

☐ **THE DECAMERON by Giovanni Boccaccio translated by Mark Musa and Peter Bondanella.** Introduction by Thomas C. Bergin. In this exuberant new translation, two scholars present a *Decameron* that speaks in contemporary *American* English, yet remains "remarkably faithful to the original in both letter and spirit . . . The reader may be assured that he is, though in another tongue, truly reading *The Decameron*."—from Thomas Bergin's Introduction. (621344—$5.95)*

*Prices slightly higher in Canada
